THE NARCOTECH
REVOLUTION

The Narcotech Revolution

A Guide to Profiting from Global Drug Reform

Hugh T. MacKenzie

DEDICATION

For my late parents, Roddy and Sheila MacKenzie.

Table of Contents

Preface

London, UK. 31 October 2022.

This book is intended as a provocative polemic essay, a non-party political pamphlet that aspires to instigate positive action. A movement of sorts, that can promote a sensible common purpose.

It is intentionally brief, avoiding jargon, citations, detail, and statistics wherever possible. There are plenty of other sources of this type of information. It aims to be accessible to the broadest possible international audience, be they knowing or naive, young or old, rich or poor, socially conservative or liberal. Likewise, its analysis and recommendations are intended for global application.

It is radical but not progressive in the modern woke sense. Personally, I am a liberty-loving free-marketeer, but one who recognizes the valid role of government and regulation in maintaining the integrity of systems, protecting the vulnerable and restraining the reckless.

Readers, family, and acquaintances may be curious as to why I have chosen to write this book and what my own qualifications to do so are. Intoxicating drugs and related criminality are an unsavory subject, and my professional background is commercial rather than academic, legal or related to law enforcement.

I took a degree in Economics and Industrial Studies from Leeds University, and have since worked with consumer-centric IT and marketing campaign management systems for most of the last twenty-five years, spanning marketing consultancy, financial services, retailing, travel, loyalty, and a lot of telecoms.

My curiosity about intoxicants and their social impact has been consistent since childhood. The topic has complexity, hypocrisy, money, and, unfortunately, violence. My own indulgences have provided fun and laughter but have also been personally challenging at times. On balance, I have been lucky but recognize that many others have been much less so.

Combined with personal experiences of people and situations accumulated over four decades or so, I am certain that there is massive global failure concerning drug policy in practice, in both the geographic and all-encompassing senses.

Hopefully this book can stimulate some debate about the opportunities available to take corrective action.

Hugh MacKenzie

Introduction

Sunset Boulevard, Los Angeles. Easter Sunday 2022

A disheveled young woman staggers into the stationary traffic backed up at traffic lights heading east on a sunny spring late afternoon. Slim and of mixed race, she is probably in her early twenties, but looks older. Almost certainly homeless, she has matted grown-out hair and, is wearing a dirt-streaked light brown t-shirt. Her dark cargo-pant trousers have slipped halfway down her thighs. Her facial expression looks vacant as she touches an SUV for support. The driver notices and maneuvers forwards slightly. The woman stands taller, scratching herself randomly, oblivious to the waiting vehicles. Slowly she walks back to the fenced sidewalk. The lights change and the vehicles accelerate away.

-

There are few things in modern life as universal as addiction. Virtually everyone on the planet uses some of the range of psychoactive substances that can alter (improve) their state of consciousness. From coffee to fentanyl, everyone wants to get high.

The good news is that disruptive change for the better is not only possible but inevitable – only the speed is open to question. The motivation? Profit. In every sense of the word, both financial and social.

Narcotech is a philosophy that says the consensual application of technologies can radically improve the outcomes arising from inherently risky substance use, helping all parties involved. Applied carefully, it can support the successful re-regulation of problematic substances.

Substance use has so far largely eluded the progress in tech that can be seen in virtually all other aspects of modern life. There are no sophisticated devices or apps that 'know' your personal history, can be linked to health care providers, and assist consumers to take better decisions.

We have barely scratched the surface of the ultra-personalized services that could be tailored to individuals. Privacy and security concerns are valid but there is value to be created in fixing them. The motives of legitimate providers are honorable – this is not basic dark web commerce run for the benefit of criminals.

The global numbers are vast. Despite falling popularity, there are still a billion or more people regularly puffing away on tobacco cigarettes[1], while billions of adults take pleasure from beers, wines, and spirits.[2] Illegal drugs like cannabis[3] and cocaine are consumed by hundreds of millions for fun, despite their prohibited status. Further millions are reluctant users due to involuntary addiction.

Global attempts at the side effects and treatment of addiction have been a mess. There are too many losers, not enough winners and too many unscrupulous beneficiaries. The financial, human and social costs have escalated out of control. There must be a change.

The core idea of this book is that there is the potential for revolutionary progress to be achieved on an evolutionary basis over a decade or so. Different tactics and strategies would be adopted at different paces, in different administrative regions, at different times, on a test and learn basis.

The rewards for success (the profits) are two-fold: substantial financial rewards for those who engineer improved outcomes but, more importantly, game-changing social change for all. These latter will be measurable in improved personal health, reduced criminality, and increased productivity, among many other benefits.

The same forces that have upended industries as diverse as taxis (e.g. Uber) and retail (e.g. Amazon) are poised to help mend broken regulatory systems that are crying out for repair and redesign. The microchip and the networked power of the Internet can empower ordinary citizens to transform their own health and relationships with wider society, whilst greatly reducing the power and significance of crime.

These are bold claims but attainable in less than a decade – and likely faster in many instances.

The prospect of reform is challenging – where to start, what needs doing, what is socially acceptable? One thing is certain, however, despite the fears of many: it doesn't mean enabling a free-for-all of selfish behavior and unfettered capitalism. After all, that is what we have rather too much of currently.

Crucially, the deciding factors will be the appetite for embracing greater responsibility (both personal and corporate) and the speed at which an informed approach to self-regulation is adopted. Above all, risks need to be far better assessed and priced accordingly, so that better quality decisions can be taken by all involved parties – whether individuals, businesses, or agencies of government.

Educational efforts to prevent the young (and others) from starting to use drink, tobacco, or drugs are laudable and not to be discounted. However, the reality is that human curiosity means many, indeed most, people will at some point make personal choices that expose them to both risk and pleasure, however momentary.

The benefits of pursuing personal pleasure can be easily understood by all, but the associated risks much less so – particularly for novice users of a substance and the young. The consequences routinely stretch beyond the individual to their families, too. Most adults know of people in their network of family and acquaintances who have struggled (or worse) with drugs, tobacco or alcohol. Legacy effects typically persist, even if an immediate addiction problem is successfully addressed.

The costs of addiction are massive for both legal and illegal drugs, and are almost never borne by those that profit most from them. Authoritarians and populist politicians exploit the demand for harsh criminal justice systems, oppressive policing, and incarceration of offenders despite the huge financial expense. In practice the results are paltry, and such policies have waning support from the general public.

Innocent victims pay the cost of drug-related property and personal crime, much of which is never satisfactorily resolved. The addicted – typically with exhausted personal reserves – look to public and charitable bodies to fund treatment that is resource-intensive and extremely profitable[4] for a few, but from which relapse is all too frequent.

Whether a psychoactive substance is new or old, near-natural or designed in a laboratory, we need much better control over them. Yet at present we are neglecting our capability to do so. At a time when human knowledge and know-how are growing exponentially, we are failing to let loose the power of IT and the microchip to aid solving one of our most pressing challenges. This is despite there being more sources of potential investment for such profitable and socially responsible projects than ever before.

Consumers can and must take greater personal responsibility for making choices that improve the consequences of their actions, assisted by information and services that, while not currently available to them, are within easy reach. Variations on the concept of personal licensing, such as voluntary or compulsory membership-type communities, will empower them as key stakeholders in a transformed relationship between the individual citizen and the state.

Working solutions, once established may be copied or adapted from territory to territory according to local conditions. What really matters is that progress could be made much, much faster than at present – greatly reducing otherwise intractable social problems, protecting human capital, respecting personal freedoms, ensuring responsibilities are adhered to, all the while generating good quality jobs and long-term investments. In sum, getting better value for money.

***

The fear of addiction has loomed large in the popular imagination for centuries. Meanwhile those with power over communities – rulers, governments, civil servants, and institutions such as the United Nations – have long seen the easy potential for raising revenues through taxing addictive substances. The more paternalistic among them worry about the potential subversion of public order and public health goals, too.

Historically, controls have come from the top down, with policies driven by a heady mix of public opinion, international obligations[5], political lobbying groups, and pure economic self-interest. Governments attempt, as best they can, to control the production, distribution, and use of intoxicating substances – categorizing them as either licit (legal) or illicit (illegal).

Possession and consumption by adults are suppressed using taxation and legal restrictions. Taxes and sanctions usually work well to shape the behavior of businesses and other formal bodies, with legal remedies available for breaches of corporate good behavior. But not always. The opioid crisis in the USA has seen such remedies take tragically far too long to be successfully applied to the bad actors. The system has eventually functioned, but too late for many victims[6].

Tax and legal compliance by individual citizens, meanwhile, can be far more variable and prone to personal choice, even when there is the awareness of risk. Many individuals – both users and dealers – are willing to break laws perceived as unjust or unlikely to be enforced. The financial rewards alone are a powerful motivator, stimulating crime, and encouraging the deeply corrosive corruption of all involved.

The failure to impose control often leads to still harsher tactics by authorities – regularly with crucial lessons left unlearned. For example, the failed experience of alcohol prohibition in the USA in the 1920s, when the production and supply of alcohol was constitutionally banned on public morality grounds[7], did not prevent the subsequent demonization of cannabis and other substances.

Prohibitionist drug policies have been copied around the world via the mechanism of United Nations Conventions, with little international variation. The 20th-century policy approach, skewed towards controlling supply, is still in place. Society is stuck in a rut, ploughing the same furrow even though the simplistic solutions of locking people up and applying 'sin' taxes has demonstrably not worked well in practice. With data and knowledge about real demand patterns universally terrible[8] (even for legal substances), it is easier for authorities to stick with tried and tested supply-control methods. But it's really a case of repeatedly kicking the can along the road.

Clearly, a rebalance is necessary and a policy upgrade needed.

A new 21st-century approach should emphasize controlling and influencing consumer demand. Politicians and regulators pay lip service to this, but do so from a prohibitionist viewpoint. Their current policy toolkits leave little room for individuals to make their own informed choices. This needs to change. Authoritarian governments like emerging surveillance technologies and will have few qualms about mandating their subjects' compliance.[9] The continued growth of surveillance will be one of the defining features of the near future.

Policy-makers have always faced difficult choices, but prohibitions in particular make it easy to institutionalize poor outcomes, globally and locally. Engaging reverse-gear rarely happens. However, it is consensual participation in policy reform that ensures democratic accountability. Far better for informed citizens to take control of their own affairs, rather than have regulation imposed upon them.

Consider a truly vulnerable group, one that all of us could find ourselves part of one day: those needing strong pain relief for end-of-life palliative care. Suffering in agony with only days or hours to live, people face a geographic lottery as to whether the authorities in their countries permit doctors to prescribe the most appropriate medications. The answer for far too many people around the world – perhaps the majority – is a straightforward 'No'. A dogmatic approach to international control regulations trumps all other considerations.[10]

As has always been the case, informed private citizens are best placed to know what is best for them. They just need lots of help to capture and process their own personal data, and to share that information which they judge necessary. Properly empowered, the individual can take much greater responsibility for themselves and make well-informed decisions.

For illegal drugs, as time passes, the global situation deteriorates. Crime has exploded, with illegal actors quick to exploit emerging technology. Witness the growth of dark web commerce mimicking legitimate retailers, the use of encrypted communications systems,[11] the shift to manufacturing synthetic compounds,[12] the use of ubiquitous social media[13], and nimbler delivery services to exploit new and younger markets.

As a result, it has never been easier to obtain illicit drugs worldwide, at a younger age, and at ever lower real prices.[14] Meanwhile, the range of substances available has expanded, becoming increasingly potent and risky to consume.

The situation is woeful. So, what needs to change? What is the roadmap?

Part One of this book deals with the status quo, outlining why we regulate as we do today, looking in detail at the consequent harms we inflict on ourselves, and examining the political and public appetite for change.

Part Two introduces in greater depth the concept of personal licensing and self-regulation. It explains how greater personal responsibility and the pricing of risk will help businesses create value-added products and services.

Part Three explains how raw data streams can be turned into information of value, while protecting civil liberties, as well as maximizing the pace of change and the range of innovators.

Part Four describes how progress can be made immediately, by applying narcotech principles to licit tobacco, nicotine, alcohol, and cannabis, as a prelude to further change.

Finally, the **Conclusion** envisages what the pace of change is likely to be over the next decade, its impact on business, and who may be the relative winners and losers.

Five key points

- Global drug policy is stuck using 20th century methods to tackle 21st century issues

- The Internet and the microchip are being massively under-utilized

- Narcotech can radically improve outcomes from risky behavior

- Success means legitimate financial profits and game-changing social benefits

- Consumers must take personal responsibility, not just rely on government to supervise supply

Part 1: The Status Quo

How we got here

- Why we have problems, what they are and how we are coping

The architecture of modern-day drug control was set by the 1961 United Nations Single Convention on Narcotic Drugs, with subsequent Conventions in 1971 and 1988 extending its regulatory reach. Building on earlier attempts to control opium in particular, the treaties are concerned with controlling the cultivation, production, and distribution of specific drugs, and their regulation for medical and scientific purposes. It is a framework that effectively splits psychotropic substances, those that affect a person's mental state, into two bands: the licit and the illicit.

Unfortunately, the UN and its subsidiary agencies are no longer the enlightened and dynamic institutions conceived of by their founders in the post-Second World War period. Meant to be forces for good, in many ways these institutions are currently exacerbating the global drug problem. They are notorious for bureaucracy, glacial decision-taking, and political squabbles, with reputations for being strongly influenced by the most conservative and authoritarian member countries, such as Russia, China and Singapore.

It seems almost unbelievable now, but worldwide medical research into psychoactive substances was heavily discouraged by design for decades from the late 1960s.[15] This was initially at the instigation of US politicians and enabling UN agencies, fallout from the tumultuous cultural wars of the late 1960s. Psychedelic evangelists such as Timothy Leary were feared to be undermining society with their advocacy of the benefits of self-exploration via drugs.

It remains the case today, worldwide, that the ability of researchers to address legitimate scientific questions is restricted by excessive compliance costs and bureaucratic traps that discourage progress.[16] The security requirements alone involved in obtaining and storing licensed versions of well-known substances are onerous, contributing to raising costs to many multiples of those paid by illegal consumers. In the USA, federal scheduling restrictions continue to hinder medical research into cannabis,[17] despite it being available for retail sale in many states.

Regulatory leeway is granted to some notable exceptional substances, characteristically minimally-processed or naturally-occurring products in widespread use in Western society for centuries. Alcohol, tobacco, tea, coffee, and, arguably, sugar, all fall into this category, but neither opium nor coca leaf do. This is despite, for instance, the coca leaf being historically widely used by indigenous populations in South America.

By contrast, the stream of refined and synthetic psychoactive products that have tumbled out of laboratories since the late-nineteenth century are all now under tight international legal controls. The default regulatory position in the UK, for instance, is to suppress and repress the usage of any new psychoactive substance, [18] with exceptions made for medical purposes.

Historically, refining opium led to morphine and heroin, while refining the coca leaf led to cocaine. Chemistry has also given rise to purely synthetic drugs including opioids like fentanyl and OxyContin, plus various types of amphetamines, benzodiazepines such as Valium, LSD and MDMA ('Ecstasy' / 'Molly') among many others. Many of the lab-derived drugs have dual purposes, with both recreational and medical applications. While combatting disease or illness was usually their primary use, secondary benefits such as bringing about euphoria, increased energy, or visions are prized by recreational consumers.

In reality, illicitly-available substances are usually much more complex than their basic chemical formulations. Ever more dangerous cocktails[19] are inadvertently created as a result of manufacturing impurities and adulteration with bulking agents.[20] Amateur chemists use whatever they can lay their hands on to stretch the profitability of their basic supplies, mixing and matching as they see fit as a substance passes through the supply chain. By the time a gram of illicit cocaine powder reaches the end consumer, it is a Frankenstein product, irrespective of what its vendors might claim.

***

A recent renaissance in research into the possible therapeutic benefits – due to their psychoactive qualities – of psychedelic and other drugs shows promise. Although religion remains a powerful social and moral force in many countries, it is the scientific method – in search of hard facts and immutable laws of nature – that underpins global economic growth. Scientific papers are being produced at an accelerated pace by academics at top-ranking universities such as Imperial College, London. Early progress has been made with respect to a range of mental health conditions and other afflictions, including addiction.[21] Substances under research around the world besides cannabis include MDMA, ketamine, psilocybin mushrooms,[22] mescaline, ibogaine[23], and kratom.[24] The pharmaceutical industry can now commercialize treatments based on new intellectual property if it can be patented. However, there is no doubt that some of this knowledge could have been acquired years ago if a less hostile operating environment had prevailed.

The study of psychoactive substances – an area where much remains to be learned – is being led by the psychiatric profession, supported by practitioners in general medicine, psychology, biology and economics. Psychiatry is a rapidly evolving specialism. In the United States, the *Diagnostic and Statistical Manual of Mental Disorders*,[25]

Fifth Edition (DSM-5) sets out criteria to assess addiction and dependence by defining and scaling substance use disorders. These disorders sit amongst a broad and rapidly expanding range of mental condition definitions.

What is often forgotten is how little we *do* know with any certainty. In the case of mental health and psychoactive substance use, the accumulated understandings of the workings of the brain, mind, and consciousness likely represent just the tip of an iceberg.

The fear of personal loss of control is at the root cause of our concern around drugs. When this loss of control extends over time – that is to say, when we are said to be addicted or dependent on a substance rather than simply temporarily intoxicated – this fear is compounded. Even if an individual may feign indifference to their own plight, society remains concerned for them, either through their family members, their physician or a paternalistic government.

Dependence is not in itself a bad thing. We are all, for example, dependent on food and water, whilst diabetics depend on insulin. Long-term dependence on an intoxicating substance need not necessarily be cause for concern, but often is. Thus, responsible physicians take great care when prescribing dependence-forming painkillers. Following malpractice suits and the opioid crisis in the USA, regulators now pay especially close attention to this area, arguably to the detriment of patient care.[26]

The term 'addiction' needs some clarification because of its commonplace and often flippant use in everyday discourse. One of the most useful definitions considers it as a simultaneous combination of dependence and harm.[27]

'Harm' is itself a very broad term. The consumption of psychoactive substances is intended primarily to impact the mental state, but clearly there are potential undesirable social outcomes of this, such as drinking-driving, family breakdown, or harm to the unborn. There are also potential harms, both mental and physical, to the user that can be directly attributed to their substance use. We know, for example, that excessive alcohol consumption can cause liver damage, while psychoactive substances can cause psychological conditions such as cravings through to serious psychiatric illnesses, such as psychosis. Moreover, physical damage to the user's body, including their brain, may result from particular consumption methods, dosing errors, and substance adulteration.

Just as the line dividing the dual medical and recreational functions of some substances can be vague and subjective, so too can be the demarcation between addiction, dependence and mere common habit. In isolation, it is comparatively straightforward to design strategies and tactics to combat direct physical harm, but complex mental and indirect social harms are far less tangible, making the policy challenge vastly more complicated.

The harm reduction movement has tried to help consumers to make better quality choices given the prevailing circumstances. Originally a pragmatic healthcare response to 1980s concerns about the HIV threat to intravenous drug users,[28] the movement has had some success in changing how drug use and users are perceived in societies that have permitted their work. Practitioners nowadays continue to try to mitigate the risks of illicit drug consumption, working around the laws in place, focusing primarily on the most marginalized substance users.

It is very much a medical and non-judgmental approach to the current drugs situation, enthusiastically backed by many drug policy reformers. Non-profits provide clean needles and promote general health, but also, for example, provide testing strips[29] for street drugs, distribute naloxone overdose survival kits, and advocate for the decriminalization of drug possession[30] and the establishment of medically-supervised safe consumption spaces. Demands for their services continue to grow and they struggle everywhere to obtain funding,[31] be it public or private.

Even with funding, the scaling of services is challenging and not always the most effective use of resources, even if popular with some supporters. For instance, mass spectrometry drug-testing services at music festivals[32] and safe consumption spaces can surely only be interim solutions that help a lucky few.

Even in a well-regulated world there would undoubtedly be a continued general need for harm reduction services, but it is the case that much current harm reduction activity is about applying a sticking plaster to serious wounds.

Regulators in democracies have to manage an extremely complex range of stakeholders, inevitably watering down the range of workable options and increasing the attractiveness of simple, blanket prohibitionist policies. However, what can be made to work for businesses concerning production and distribution does not do so well for end-use consumers and the otherwise innocent general public. In the next section we will see just how poor the overall outcomes are from the current regulatory architecture.

Five key points

- Existing frameworks to control supply and demand need upgrading for complexities of 21st century life

- Regulators are extremely uncomfortable about recreational intoxication

- Scientific and medical knowledge is growing at pace, but much remains to be understood

- Addiction and dependence are human issues being addressed on a fire-fighting basis

- The medical profession is doing the heavy lifting on very complex social issues

The costs of failure

- The size of the prize, current problems and opportunities to gain

An astute government or other body responsible for drawing up regulations – of anything, not just drugs – is seeking to design a system that maximizes its intended benefits, with the fewest possible shortcomings. Perfection is unlikely and there will always be comparative winners and losers, so the political challenge is to manage these trade-offs to find an optimal outcome for society. This includes helping an individual to protect themselves from their own behavioral decisions.

In the context of psychoactive substances, the three key consumer regulatory objectives are: to protect individuals from the harms of actual substances themselves; to restrain the activities of the suppliers or businesses providing substances, if needed; and to protect society from the impact of individuals choosing to take substances.

In practice, these objectives overlap but can be assessed by considering their impact on human capital, whether the criminal justice system is functioning as intended, whether regulations are having perverse outcomes, and whether society is helping or hindering those in the greatest need. On each of these measures, we shall see that the ordinary citizen is being shortchanged by current regulatory systems. The financial, human and social costs have escalated out of control, yet society seems powerless to rectify the situation.

Addiction and dependence are personal afflictions, though with prospective impacts beyond the individual. Measuring consequences such as the impact on the individual's health, wellbeing and productivity is extremely challenging, especially in the absence of high-quality information systems. As the maxim goes, if you can't measure it, you can't manage it.

Regulators in the drugs field are interested in the impact on human capital, an individual's capacity to participate and contribute to society. A person struggling with addiction is probably losing capital; a contented person may be accumulating human capital.

Raising drugs education and awareness, in particular for the young, is a worthy endeavor and meets two of the three regulatory objectives outlined above. As an attempt to protect human capital, few will argue with the principal of reducing use and preventing or at least delaying initiation into substance use, even if some may debate the specific content of particular messages.

Across the public and non-profit sectors, there is a great deal of reliance on education. It is accessible, visible and the inputs at least are comparatively easy to measure and report on.[33] The outputs – the successes and failures – are far less so, however.

Human capital is the ultimate resource, and there is one Key Performance Indicator that is less subjective than most: deaths. Those directly attributable to overdose or poisoning are relatively clear-cut; deaths due to the long-term consequences of normal consumption, say for tobacco, are evident but of a more complex nature.

Healthcare economists try to place a financial value on missed years of life due to early death. What, for example, would an individual's contribution have been worth if they were not killed in an accident. Different rates are used in different countries, according to relative wealth. The White House's Council of Economic Advisors placed a financial value on the lives of those killed by the opioid crisis in the

USA, which during 2018 alone was put at a staggering $618 billion, or 3.4% of GDP.[34] Tragically, the annual death toll has increased further each year since,[35] suggesting the annual figure is still growing.

Not all psychoactive substance consumption is problematic, but it is worth considering its global scale. The world's billion-plus tobacco smokers, for example, risk considerable harms from their ongoing consumption, including the significant risk of reduced life expectancy and serious illnesses.[36] Then there is alcohol. Rates of alcohol consumption vary dramatically even within regions such as Europe, according to local culture. But more than half of the adult population of the Americas, Europe and the Western Pacific region (including China) will have consumed alcohol in the last year,[37] with substantially lower levels in the Muslim world and South Asia. The World Health Organization, a United Nations agency, estimates that some three million deaths per year are attributable to harmful alcohol use, 5.3% of all deaths,[38] with alcohol consumption linked to more than 200 disease and injury conditions.

In some cities, wastewater analysis by scientists provides insight into population-level substance use and trends.[39] However, in general the absence of good quality consumer-centric data means that statistics concerning the bulk of countries – whether wealthy or poor – are very rough estimates. Nevertheless, the United Nations Office on Drugs and Crime's World Drug Report does attempt to collate the data each year. Its *2022 World Drug Report*[40] reported the following estimated numbers of users in 2020: Cannabis, 220 million; Opioids (including opiates and prescription opioids), 61 million; Opiates alone, 31 million; Cocaine-type products, 21 million; Amphetamines including methamphetamine, 34 million; "Ecstasy", 20 million.

The scale of these estimates highlights the obvious inadequacy of the criminal justice systems that are attempting to suppress use via coercion. That so many individuals are prepared to risk the consequences of criminalization brings into question both the basic efficacy of such an approach, and whether it is desirable on any level to marginalize such substantial proportions of the adult populations.

The marginalization of illicit drug users has done untold damage to communities across the world, creating vast fearful underclasses that might otherwise be aligned with the authorities. The boundaries between the lawful many and the lawless few are needlessly blurred, while the repercussions from non-malevolent errors and mistakes can last a lifetime.

This is not, by any means, a reason to excuse the very real crimes that broader society suffer as a consequence of the illegal drug trade worldwide. Shoplifting, burglaries, robberies, and muggings are driven by the need of illicit drug users to finance otherwise unsustainable habits, transferring a massive cost burden to the general population, needlessly increasing insecurity and reducing quality of life.

More serious crime, including homicides and political corruption, is endemic in societies that lack the institutional capacity to contain the influence of drug-trade gangsters. Over the last two decades in Mexico alone, tens of thousands of people have lost their lives as a consequence of the operations of the illegal drug industry.[41] Many have been innocent bystanders or members of the media attempting to chronicle events.[42]

Everywhere, law enforcement personnel are particularly at risk. They work with the ever-present threat of personal harm as they carry out their professional duties, while lucrative opportunities for corruption tempt many.[43]

The illicit drug user numbers are indicative of the size of the black market opportunities available to those who wish to pursue them, and of the armies of criminals and gangs involved in supply and distribution. The unscrupulous and dangerous are attracted to this business, and virtually without exception are wholly unsuited to taking a responsible approach. These are not people with the skills and qualifications of, for instance, trained pharmacists or supermarket-buyer teams.

Popular culture and the media ascribe a level of sophistication to black market operators that is rarely grounded in reality. Ostentatious displays of wealth, lurid tales of excess, grossly-inflated street values, and simplistic smuggling-route infographics belie the reality of life in cartels, mafias and gangs. These are simple, brutish businesses where extraordinary profits mask perennial problems, including short-termism, high-cost structures, constrained labor pools, ineptitude, and the ever-present risk of threats from competitors, law enforcement and taxation authorities. [44]

Production, international trafficking, wholesale and most street-level dealing are clearly commercial activities, with violence or the implicit threat of violence the arbiter of disputes. There is little doubt about the motives of those involved and there is rightly little public sympathy for the few that are disrupted by law enforcement. The cavalier approach to laws, regulations and social niceties impacts end- customers too – production techniques are informal and slack, quality controls poor to non-existent, and adulteration typically a fundamental part of the business model. [45]

At the very end of distribution chains, the demarcations between simple possession and supply offences are often fluid. This vastly expands the numbers of those complicit in providing illicit drugs to others. One of the most pernicious features of drug prohibition is that it encourages and perpetuates the user-dealer model. User-dealers expand the reach of distribution channels by selling to friends and acquaintances, often in order to subsidize their own consumption habits. [46] The network effect of such social-supply can be seen across all types of illicit drugs, deepening the corrosive corruption and criminalization of those whose involvement might otherwise be more limited.

Not only are taxpayers around the world forgoing tax revenues from illicit substances, but they are paying to maintain ineffective enforcement schemes that support the profits of criminal activity at levels far higher than was envisaged when the relevant laws were conceived. Established suppliers on both sides of the legal divide, gradually become vested interests that prefer to perpetuate the status quo for commercial reasons.

Being able to levy and collect taxes on psychoactive substances can be problematic in itself, as is well known with tobacco and alcohol. Just as individuals can become dependent on a substance, a government can display indications of addiction to a particularly lucrative revenue stream.[47] The temptation to raise taxes on goods where demand is not sensitive to price is strong, but runs the risk of encouraging black markets and their associated social costs. There is a sweet spot, but it is rarely hit.

Australia now has the most expensive tobacco products in the world[48] due to the continued rapid escalation of tax rates so as to discourage consumption. Legal demand has dipped but price levels are now so high that industrial-scale smuggling of cigarettes from abroad risks jeopardizing both public health goals and compliance with national and state laws.[49] Die-hard smokers are unconvinced about the benefits to them of increased regulation, which in their view is excessive.[50]

Jurisdictions now legalizing forms of cannabis are struggling to strike a balance between desired taxation levels and the ease with which consumers can revert to still widely available black-market products.[51]

In most countries, smokers and drinkers find it comparatively easy to turn to health professionals and self-help groups such as Alcoholics Anonymous, assuming they can afford to do so and are sufficiently motivated. Rehabilitation schemes driven by governments and law enforcement have historically had fearsome reputations in some countries, though some enlightened progress is being made.[52]

Despite addiction problems having been serious social issues for many decades, there are few simple solutions and the science is not well developed. The rehab and treatment sector are characterized by fragmentation, uncertainty, relapse, and, above all, by cost. Each of these problems is magnified for those addictions that families and consumers fear the most. They are also exacerbated by the illegal status of the substances in question.[53]

For stimulant addiction, such as to cocaine and crack, there is a paucity of effective pharmacological options to reduce or stop cravings.[54] Opioid and opiates have a much broader range of treatment options but many involve long-term medical supervision. [55] Stabilization of the most chaotic of illicit drug users on medically-prescribed preparations has short-term merits. There is a historic[56] and current[57] evidence base that provides some support for it. Unsurprisingly, it is popular with users who can resume more normal law-abiding existences,[58] even if compliance conditions apply.

The problem is, what constitutes the short-, medium- or long-term for any given individual?

Parents and others with pastoral responsibilities are amongst the most concerned.

Irrespective of claimed medical or social benefits, the mass of the general public has strong opinions about many drug consumption behaviors, whether conducted in private or not. Drunkenness, vaping, tobacco smoke and the reek of cannabis are considered at best a nuisance by non-participants. Specialist pipes, the snorting of powders, and intravenous injection are taboo.

Frequently the personal circumstances of an individual user are complicated by usage of multiple substances, compounded by other medical conditions, be they physical or mental.[59] The desperate plight of many of the visible homeless on the streets of the West Coast of the USA shows what can happen in the absence of functioning social safety nets.[60]

The financing of addiction support on an on-going basis from the public purse has practical limitations and is hugely unpopular with voters,[61] even when the will of administrators is present. Insurers, too, are financially constrained.[62] For those with acute addiction problems, recovery goals must either be abstinence or the interim adoption of self-funded, less harmful substitutes.

Psychiatric care is a scarce and, hence, extremely expensive resource.[63] The gold standard of residential rehab care, if that is what is required, is exceptionally costly and labor-intensive. Neither are available or within the reach of most people around the globe. Coverage by health insurance schemes in wealthy countries is far from universal and stories abound of families self-funding expensive treatment of loved ones.[64]

In the USA in particular, exploitation by rehabilitation operators is widespread,[65] a situation not helped by the patchwork of services and information available. Well-known providers of services to troubled celebrities, for instance, are not representative of the broader industry, serving rather to highlight the variance in treatment and its effectiveness.

There is a pressing need to dramatically raise the efficacy and professional standards of the treatment sector in all countries. The funding challenge, meanwhile, will ultimately have to be met by the development of new, cheaper and more efficient treatments, which will enable more people to be more quickly 'cured' for the same amount of resource input.

This is something that can only be done in an environment where individuals have access to better personal information. Before looking at how this can be achieved in Parts 2 and 3, we first need to understand the political context for change.   -

Five key points

- Neither law enforcement nor public health approaches to addiction are providing acceptable results

- There is a deficit of personal-level information – we measure what we can, rather than what we need to know

- Crime and corruption are corrosive to the many involved, as well as subverting social order on a disproportionate scale

- Treatment and rehabilitation needs are not being well met anywhere. Funding and efficacy are extremely problematic.

- Drug regulation is laboring with techniques designed for the last century

The politics of drug reform

- Why society is poised for change if it's sold successfully

Fashions come and go, not least those concerning psychoactive substances.

Coffee, tea, and sugar are now familiar mainstream commodities that attract little specific taxation or regulation. However, historically, the simplicity of applying taxes to what were once scarce, highly desirable products kept prices high and made smuggling exceedingly lucrative.

Attitudes to tobacco have fluctuated since it was introduced into Europe in the sixteenth century. More than one ruler has tried to legislate it out of existence in their country in the intervening years, starting with King James I of England in 1604.[66] Mass-produced branded cigarettes, now in terminal decline, are a comparatively recent phenomenon that followed factory automation. Women only became a significant consumer group in the twentieth century.[67]

The relative sobriety of the customers of the coffee shops that emerged in seventeenth-century European commercial centers like London, Amsterdam, and Antwerp was novel in and of itself. At the time, most people's diet contained a great deal of weak beer, which was nutritious and safer to drink than the available water supplies.[68]

The clear-headed stimulant effects of caffeine on the coffee drinkers contrasted with the typically depressant effects of alcohol on the general population. Such coffee shops were the scandalous drug consumption rooms of their day. Gossiping customers were presumed to be planning and scheming to undermine the existing social order.

Several of the refined chemicals that give rise to the greatest concern today – notably morphine, heroin and cocaine – were once legally available and marketed freely to the general public as active ingredients in patent medicine concoctions.[69] It is widely known that Coca-Cola, perhaps the most famous drinks brand in the world, contained cocaine as one of its key ingredients in the 1890s.[70] Less well known is that deactivated coca leaf is still used to flavor Coke today.[71]

Before the discovery of morphine and cocaine later in the nineteenth century, the Opium Wars took place between 1839–42 and 1856–60. Remarkable as it may seem today, the British state exploited its then global naval dominance to force opium products on a largely unsophisticated and vulnerable Chinese population.[72]

Among the consequences were that Hong Kong was established as a trading post, while buccaneering British companies made great fortunes. But mass opium addiction was the result in mainland China. Most Westerners are oblivious to or know little about these episodes, but the Opium Wars are seared into the memories of the Chinese public today.[73]

Moving into the early twentieth century, a press-led moral panic[74] led to the gradual introduction of restrictions on patent medicine products. Racism was a contributory factor, particularly towards Chinese immigrants in San Francisco who were believed to be spreading the opium habit.[75] In subsequent decades, overt racist stereotypes were used in other press-led panics focused on Mexicans and cannabis,[76] and cocaine and Black people.[77]

Minorities tend not to fare well in most political and social systems, and aside from caffeine and alcohol, the use of psychoactive substances is a distinctly minority pursuit in most countries and regions. Consumers are vulnerable to the whims, tolerance and concerns of larger, otherwise non-involved sections of the population. However, these minorities often also need protecting from themselves.

There is an economic rule of thumb called the Pareto Principle,[78] named after the nineteenth century Italian economist, David Pareto. This holds that 80% of consequences are accounted for by 20% of the causes. It works for much psychoactive drug consumption, where dependent people use a lot more than more numerous casual users and may also have their own special regulatory needs (as highlighted in the analysis[79] of Professor Jonathan Caulkins of Carnegie Mellon University).

A neat illustration of this point can be made with reference to cannabis consumers, although the principle applies to alcohol drinkers too. The incidence of dependence and psychiatric illness amongst the relatively few people who smoke cannabis daily is thought to be higher than in the much larger population who smoke only occasionally. Policy-makers concerned with the whole market need to consider the mental health implications of the small subset of heavy smokers against freedom-seeking demands from the larger group.[80]

Not every lawmaker is interested in protecting the interests of minorities versus majorities. Policy-makers, whether or not in democracies, are susceptible to being swayed by interpretations of the will of the people.

In modern times, mass media – such as radio, television, and newspapers – both use and steer public opinion, consciously or otherwise. The rise of social media and the fragmentation of traditional media channels has made public opinion increasingly fluid and subject to rapid change. This is measured and publicized by a polling industry that tries to tease out trends over time. There is an in-built tendency to polarize debate and to simplify complex nuance into 'yes' or 'no'-style perspectives.[81]

In the case of illicit drugs, these two poles are represented by prohibitionists and liberalizers. Although seemingly at opposite ends of the spectrum, passionate liberalizers and die-hard prohibitionists have more in common than might be immediately apparent. The very fact of their activism indicates that they care about the global illicit drug problem and its impact on them, their families, and community institutions.

The liberalizers draw parallels with historic wrongs such as colonialism and racial injustice,[82] and argue that they are armed with data-backed evidence and knowledge. In their mind, the prohibitionists are paternalistic and make disproportionate use of the coercive powers of the modern state. The prohibitionists, by contrast, are convinced that they hold the moral high-ground, protecting society from reckless liberalizers armed with the seeds of their own self-destruction.[83]

Both sides are boxed in by paradoxical situations. Many prohibitionists would admit that some reform is needed, yet have their hands tied by binding international legislation. Meanwhile, liberalizers know that existing established and flourishing black markets can be a boon for consumers, for example in terms of tax-free prices and accessibility.[84]

More politically influential than both types of activists is a third (and probably largest) party: a silent majority who go with the prevailing flow. However, their relative indifference can evaporate quickly with a change in personal circumstances that pushes them sharply into one or other camp.

These are the people who bear most of the costs of the war on drugs – the victims of property and violent crime; those who suffer the inconvenience and expense of complying with know-your-customer and anti-money laundering regulations;[85] those whose loved-ones get arrested or addicted.

The sheer numbers of families impacted by the devastating synthetic opioid crisis in North America has dramatically escalated the importance of drug dependence issues across the political spectrum, but it has not reached the top of the political agenda yet. Ultimately it is a slow-motion cultural war, one creating needless real casualties. Quicker reform and greater compromise are desperately needed.

Progress includes the establishment in 2011 of the Global Commission on Drugs Policy.[86] This multi-lateral organization is made up of a cast of influential left-leaning former political leaders from around the globe, plus intellectuals and businesspeople. It has generated lengthy reports[87] available in many languages and provides vocal encouragement and support to activists. However, its actual political accomplishments to date are modest, despite the efforts to rally civil society.

Other progress has bubbled up from the grass-roots level. Drug consumption rooms have opened in many cities around the world, in a long-shot bid to reduce the tally of fatal overdoses.[88] Activists have succeeded in legalizing recreational cannabis in Canada and several US states; the German coalition government hopes to follow in 2023, EU law permitting.[89] A rush of speculative venture capital investment in both the US and Europe is looking for commercial returns from psychedelic drugs.

Regarding alcohol and tobacco, the political direction of travel is towards stricter controls, driven by creeping public health concerns about personal health issues.[90] Regulations are becoming ever more onerous and paternalistic,[91] as the intolerant and intemperate try to adopt the moral high ground using published scientific research as evidence.

There is little push-back from consumers, who typically lack the organization of either the formal bodies making the regulations or the pressure groups calling for them. Licit producers and suppliers do attempt to protect their own commercial interests but are vulnerable to charges of delaying and other forms of subterfuge.[92] There is little public sympathy for the plight of tobacco industry stakeholders.

So how does all this apply to drug policy reform? What needs to change?

The current paradigm of illicit drug control, prohibition, is simple enough to be well understood by all. If your behavior breaks the law, by supplying or possessing a banned substance, you may be punished.

Any significant new developments must enjoy similar universal comprehension and transparency of application, irrespective of wealth, educational achievement, or intelligence quotient.

This is not a criticism of the efforts of reformers to date, constrained by a legal landscape not of their choosing. Rather, it is a recognition that only a step-change can circumvent the growing difficulties of the current approach to liberalization. Few people, if any, can succinctly distinguish between efforts to legalize, decriminalize and depenalize supply, possession, or consumption of licit and illicit substances – in many instances a mixture of all.[93] There is also massive ambiguity in their application, magnifying the uncertainty of outcomes.

The solution, as we shall see in the next chapter, is to focus on changing demand by building on the widely understood concept of a licensed user.

Five key points

- Prohibitionists and liberalizers are outnumbered by those who will go with the flow

- Attitudes are polarized but compromise is possible, with some progress being made

- Minorities need protecting from members of their own group, in addition to wider society

- Consumers typically lack the organization of regulators, producers, and special interest groups

- New and existing technologies have a massive opportunity to improve outcomes for consumers and wider society

Part 2: Improving Regulation

Encouraging personal responsibility

- Why individuals must assert their rights to choose wisely

The mantra of campaigners interested in liberalizing drug policy reform is "legalize and regulate". As a slogan, it captures the essence of what is needed and has steered the objectives of change, focusing on supply and law-enforcement.

Campaigners have relied on blurring boundaries between recreational and medical consumption, then leading with demands for legal supply for medical purposes. This was the case for cannabis in those parts of North America where it can now be sourced legally for adult recreational purposes, and is a strategy likely to be repeated both for other substances like MDMA and the psychedelics.

The pace of change, however, has been glacially slow, irrespective of what both campaigners and the authorities may claim. The reality is that developments and trends in global drug markets move much faster than the legislative process, creating fresh and often more serious problems.

The key word in the last paragraph is markets. According to economists, market forces are determined by supply and demand. Governments know it, not least in the traditional producer countries most impacted by the so-called "War on Drugs".[94] Their political leaders[95] repeatedly blame demand in consumer countries[96] for causing the violence and corruption related to illicit production and trafficking.

By their very nature, most government bodies and many politicians have authoritarian tendencies. They seek to define and enforce laws that impact others. If they believe them to be effective in reducing demand, they will extend and develop the range of drug controls and sanctions.

Drug and alcohol courts are an increasing feature of many US states, complementing the rest of the criminal justice system.[97] The New Zealand government intends to prohibit the sale of tobacco to those born after 2008.[98] The United Kingdom is considering withdrawing passport and travel rights from repeat illicit drug offenders.[99]

Drug policy reformers need to be innovative concerning demand too, or risk passing the opportunity to shape the future to those with the most illiberal and authoritarian outlooks.

You don't need to be a libertarian to be worried, but it helps. Other countries may adopt or mimic the totalitarian surveillance systems already being built in China, where citizens are increasingly monitored wherever and whatever they do.[100] The Chinese social credit system may still be evolving and under constant development,[101] but who can forecast its reach and capabilities in a decade's time?[102] Today it may seem broadly analogous to Western credit-ratings systems, but many fear an Orwellian development path. Which territories will copy it?

So how should reformers of all persuasions tackle demand?

We need to go beyond simply modifying the statuses of substances, their availability, and any possible sanctions. To enable better quality personal decisions to be made, there must be at least a partial transfer of responsibilities to the individual, fueled by a revolution in the information available on which to base those decisions.

Aside from law enforcement and some areas of medical research, modern information technology has been grossly under-utilized for addressing the challenges posed by both licit and illicit intoxicating substances. In virtually every other sphere of life, the sustained exponential growth in computing power has raised living standards worldwide, creating jobs, opportunities, and general prosperity.

In the drugs context, the big opportunity is to efficiently enable the individual – or a delegated agent – to monitor and control themselves, rather than have it done to them as at present. The benefits and consequences cascade upwards, rather than downwards.

Adapting and applying the kinds of consumer-centric IT used in other areas of life, ranging from supermarkets to finance, would have a radical impact on the effectiveness of policies, both new and prospective. Moreover, progress could begin quickly, as many data constraints are contrived rather than technical.[103] An evidence base will accumulate rapidly.

The scope for innovation is huge, with financial implications for economies that extend far beyond the raising of sin tax revenues by governments. We are repeatedly told that data is the new oil. We can reasonably expect to generate new intellectual property, services, companies and jobs, creating financial and social value at every step.

Better informed individuals will hopefully take better quality decisions about their lifestyles; better informed authorities can plan and implement better policies to protect human capital. It is a utopian view of the future, one that can replace the dystopian outlook of today. Its successful adoption would be quite revolutionary in its implications.

So how do we make it happen? What is the path forward?

To answer these questions, we must start by considering the responsibilities of individuals, before considering how to improve regulation and address the civil liberties implications of harnessing new, ultra-sensitive personal data.

Five key points

- Reformers must be more innovative and focus on demand, not just supply

- Consumers must act for themselves or else have technologies applied against them

- IT can generate the evidence base for decision-taking that is missing now

- The absence of information is fixable, where there is willingness to try both the new and the already proven

- Supply controls need to work in tandem with empowered citizens, to help not hurt

Self-regulating citizens

- How individuals can both protect and hold themselves to account

It is a self-evident truism that it is individuals who consume psychoactive substances, licit or otherwise. A company or other organization cannot, for instance, become intoxicated though they may well otherwise benefit from drug consumption. Different regulations might apply for groups of people, whether formally organized or not, but certain controls can only ever be applicable for individuals at the personal level.

Laws and regulations that apply at the individual level, like those that might govern personal licensing, raise important questions about civil liberties. Freedom of choice is a fundamental human right and ordinary adults should have great agency over what they ingest into their bodies.

At the same time, as per 19th century philosopher John Stuart Mill's harm principle,[104] individuals have obligations to fellow stakeholders such as dependent family members or fellow road users. There is also a social responsibility not to unduly destroy their own personal human capital, their health, and wellbeing. The state has a valid safety-net role in protecting the most vulnerable if they can't look after their own interests.

There is a delicate balance to be struck between the civil liberties of the individual versus the powers of authorities. Mass civil disobedience, such as by those choosing to break drug possession laws, undermines the effectiveness of the entire system of law and order, and is an outcome which authorities ordinarily strive to avoid. Whenever possible, all possible efforts should be applied to keep individuals within a legal framework.

The concept of a licensed drug user does two critical things. It provides an opportunity for current law-breakers to gain the respect and protections available to regular society – for the individual to re-balance their relationship with society. To those individuals whose activities might be newly constrained, it enables society to be better able to apply the types of controls that might otherwise be done so using prohibition.

So how might drug user licensing work in practice? Who is the licensing authority? Would a personal license be voluntary or compulsory? What happens if I breach the license?

Transport is the most obvious analogy of how personal licensing might work in practice for licit substances, be they licit today or in the future. In order to drive a car on public roads, basic competence needs to be demonstrated to a licensing authority. Different, more rigorous constraints may apply to the drivers of large goods vehicles; regulations for cyclists may be much more relaxed.

There may be ongoing obligations, such as to obey speed limits while driving and not otherwise abuse or subvert the intent of the regulations. Repeated breaches of this duty of care to others may lead to sanctions and withdrawal of driving permissions.

Core to the system of control is the notion of benign centralized authorities that grant and monitor compliance on behalf of all road users.

Another widely understood type of licensing is the commercial sort that protects the intellectual property rights of creators, such software designers, movie studios, or pharmaceutical companies. By imposing usage restrictions on the intellectual property, creators can enjoy legal protections for their products and services.

Correspondingly, end-users have the right to utilize licensed products but within a defined framework that seeks to prevent prohibited uses.

For drugs, an easy visualization of personal licensing starts with a basic requirement of a purchaser needing to present some type of ID at the point of sale. From here, a wealth of possibilities opens up.

Countries or states where recreational cannabis is already legal might introduce personal licensing systems with sales tax benefits for voluntary participation. The prescription supply of opiate or opioid drugs could be conditional on compliance with usage monitoring systems, aimed at preventing social supply to others. Tobacco smokers could be compelled to register their purchases with public health authorities. Till receipts at alcohol outlets might be mandated to contain QR code visualizations of purchases.

As we shall see in the next chapter when discussing the "sinners' passport", the greatest potential benefits from narcotech will arise when data is generated and captured at the personal, individual level, enabling a single-customer view. The practicalities of whether this is anonymous or otherwise, voluntary or compulsory, will depend on jurisdictions, circumstances, specific substances, and the available point of sale and consumption-measuring technologies. Hence, the personal licensing requirements necessary to buy a box of coca tea bags[105] should be considerably less stringent than those for purchasing an MDMA tablet from a specialist retailer.[106]

In the case of motoring, it is widely accepted that a government agency is a suitable centralized authority for supervising the issuance of licenses and so on. In the case of psychoactive substances this does not naturally have to be the case. Indeed, considerable resistance to this would come from many quarters, not just from conspiracy theorists. Experience with COVID restrictions will make many wary of government involvement.

Instead, consumers themselves should step up to protect their own interests, forming membership-type communities that take responsibility for their own affairs. After all, they know what is in their own best interests and have the expertise to set reasonable standards focused on protecting the vulnerable.

Single-purpose membership communities need not be monopolies, and membership need not necessarily be limited to active users of a particular substance. Ex-users will typically have valid contributions to make.

Be they commercial or non-profit, vigorous competition between providers will improve the quality and range of services on offer, while different categories of membership can provide a voice for those that might otherwise be ignored or have particular needs.

Trade unions and professional associations provide a well-understood current-day model of how such communities can form, develop, and finance themselves.

Self-regulation of the type outlined above is entirely consistent with meeting not only the objectives of public health that might be mandated by national or state governments, but also the concerns of individuals about their civil liberties. Critically, it places greatest responsibility on those that wish to take risks, to protect both themselves and others.

By doing this, we can reasonably hope for significantly greater levels of social co-operation and compliance.

This chapter has focused on how personal licensing can create an environment in which demand-side reform can thrive. For a narcotech evolution to thrive, there is also a need for changes to the licensing and regulation of suppliers of licit substances.

Five key points

- The social and financial costs of existing control policies are substantial and increasingly unsustainable

- Drug and alcohol users are not social islands, but have responsibilities beyond themselves

- The licensed user concept is easily understood, flexible and ties personal data to an individual. Membership-type communities can support groups of individuals

- Consumer licensing can radically improve the availability of information about legal psychoactive substance use. All stakeholders can benefit

- There are a large range of potential markets and implementations around the world

Allowing business to help

- Why measuring and pricing personal risk is critical

Financial rewards and the drug problem make uneasy bedfellows at present.

In the illicit sphere, there is a populist view that the consumption of drugs, misery, crime, riches, and corruption are all closely entwined and will be ever thus. In some jurisdictions where legal restrictions have loosened in recent years, black markets remain strong and challenge campaigners' preconceptions about the desirability of further reform.

In the licit sphere of today – the world of alcohol, tobacco, and some prescription pharmaceuticals – the selling of 'sin' products sits uneasily in the minds of many voters. Industry participants typically have co-dependent relations not just with their consumers, but also with the state that regulates and taxes them.

Intoxicating substances are different and do have to be dealt with on a different basis to, for example, selling a can of beans. That doesn't, however, mean that the vast power of commerce, the magical "invisible hand",[107] cannot be leveraged to optimally allocate capital and make profits.

Many drug policy reformers have progressive or leftist viewpoints and are instinctively critical of the workings of capitalism and the free market. They desire a larger role for government in the legal production and distribution of intoxicating substances, beyond mere oversight.[108]

Though superficially attractive, this would delay the evolution of technology-based solutions that will achieve the outcomes all reformers need to work towards. The danger in concentrating responsibilities with the state and civil servants is that the pace of innovation will be slowed and new ecosystems supporting economic growth and jobs will not flourish.

There are many flaws with the commercialization of legal cannabis products in the USA, not least those related to the advertising, such as on billboards, allowed under First Amendment freedoms[109] – conduct that wouldn't be permitted in most countries. But undoubtedly, the vibrancy of the sector and the scale and sophistication of its support businesses could not have been achieved under a government-led monopoly.

New business opportunities lead to new commercial interest groups. These range from organizations wishing to grow the overall size of their customer markets as well simply gaining market share, to new professions seeking to protect their status and raise their remuneration.

Traditional medical service-providers such as physicians and pharmacists may choose to reduce their current day-to-day addiction, treatment, and dispensing responsibilities as new specialisms emerge. New professions would have greater focus on recreational consumption issues.

Licit private sector companies enjoy the full protections of the law, including the right to form trade associations in most jurisdictions, and legitimately try to influence politicians and other regulators who cover their activities. Some companies, even in newly licit sectors, may be reluctant to see the introduction of technologies that could ultimately shrink their customer bases or profitability.

Established industries are often well-funded and highly experienced at operating in regulated sectors. Delaying strategies will undoubtedly be deployed, to differing effect in different countries and regions. It will be up to national or regional regulators to assess these on their own merits, and take legislative action if required.

Focus on profit will enable capitalists to work their magic, but as in so many other fields, guardrails are necessary. This is the classic role for the state – setting a regulatory framework that incentivizes and rewards desired activities whilst monitoring for and preventing undesirable outcomes.

In tandem with the self-regulating consumer communities envisaged in the previous section, the role of light-touch but vigilant and flexible regulators can be far more influential than seen to date in existing licit sectors. The difference will be due to gaining access to demand-side data and information of a richness and quality unheard of today. Decision-taking will thus be empowered.

Likewise, insurers – an industry with a traditionally conservative outlook – will be empowered to better price the risk of consuming psychoactive substances, which ultimately may enable better quality decisions to be taken by consumers themselves.

The insurance sector can be expected to play an out-sized role in shaping how legitimate psychoactive marketplaces function. In particular, insurance premiums can act as price signals that channel product designs and encourage lower-risk consumer behaviors (just as the introduction of seat belts was reflected in the operation of the car insurance market).

A membership community might, for instance, offer specialist mental health insurance as part of a membership fee. They might also refuse to accept a prospective member without insurance coverage, or steer them to a lower tier without access to particular products.

Better understanding and pricing of risk will be hugely important to businesses across the value chain, with derivative impacts too.

Legitimate businesses seek stability, predictability, and try as far as possible to minimize risks to shareholder returns. Expensive problems such as product liability claims are minimized and avoided whenever possible.

The final, but probably most important licensing aspect to take into consideration is that of the ownership and access to the raw data created. This is a legal minefield, but the opportunities for innovation and boosting productivity hinge on it.

Supplier businesses may hope that better data – according to their access to it – means better targeting of consumers, lower sales costs, higher volumes, and improved returns. Their prospective customers will aspire to vastly improved terms of trade, being able to make informed choices, with their interests better safeguarded.

Not all freedoms will be welcomed. Should, for example, a deep-pocketed tobacco company be able to buy access to cannabis market trends?

Public health authorities might compromise about their data requirements one year, only to attempt to push through amendments another. Such changes might involve the anonymity of personally identifiable information, or an extension of permissions buried in obscure legal clauses.

What kind of institutional arrangements best protect the individual? Delegated responsibility, such as to a membership community, is virtually inevitable at some stage. Individuals will have strong feelings about the storage and digital distribution of their sensitive personally-identifiable data. The speed at which narcotech iteration happens and benefits can be banked will largely be down to the successful regulation of licit industry use of data.

At every level – personal, local, regional, international – progress will be evolutionary and varied, rather than revolutionary and standardized. What works in one place will be tried again in another, based on the value created.

Five key points

- Business can speed the evolution of services to empower citizens and regulators

- Detailed information about demand is currently absent at the individual level

- New and existing technologies can help control systems function more effectively for all

- Business can learn to understand and appropriately price the true cost of risk

- Light-touch, vigilant regulators can assist all stakeholders, preventing undesirable outcomes

Part 3: Creating Value

Monetizing raw ultra-personal data

- How to remedy and profit from the information void

Underpinning the philosophy of narcotech is the belief that raw data about consumer behavior can be collected, stored and transformed into information of value, to the benefit of all parties – an opportunity that is currently foregone.

At present, the individual consumer is their own chief data repository and processor, mostly unaided except for till receipts and any personal paperwork they might maintain. For black market transactions, the data trail will be intentionally non-existent and evidence-free. As we might imagine, the consumer's own capacity for insight and self-analysis will be limited at best.

In virtually every other aspect of modern economic life aside from psychoactive substances, commercial, government, and non-profit entities are striving to improve their relationships with customers using data, optimally achieving a single customer view of the individual in question, enabling a potential one-to-one relationship. [110]

The fashionable term for the ability to leverage a single view of a customer is Customer Value Management (CVM), a successor and derivative of the more long-standing and widely known Customer Relationship Management (CRM).

They are not simply marketing buzz terms. Organizations whose information architectures support this ability can accurately personalize communications and offers using the customer's own transaction and interaction history. Outcomes are not restricted to personalized marketing; utility billing systems, for instance, will rely on similarly precise data.

It's an obvious point to make but it needs explicitly stating: if personal data is available, personalization becomes possible. In its absence, it isn't and the opportunity is missed.

Different end-users have different needs from personalization. A customer who wishes to understand how much money or tax that they have paid over six months on cannabis products needs their own purchase data, across all of the retailers they have used in the period – when, where, what, how much they paid.

A public health researcher may need the same information, less the name and actual identity of the customer. However, instead of data for just one customer, they want it for thousands of customers so that they can aggregate, or slice and dice, the data set using an analytical tool.

Given current-day technologies in widespread use like mobile apps and QR codes, it is not difficult to conceive of new, valuable services that could be rapidly developed if more raw data was captured in a consumer-centric manner.

Such an ecosystem might stimulate novel data-capture and analysis technologies to be developed. E-cigarettes or electronic vapes, used for delivering nicotine and the active ingredients of cannabis today. have prospective 'big data' capabilities that are largely unrealized to date.

Artificial Intelligence algorithms could be deployed to influence purchase or consumption decisions – and consumers themselves may choose that they do so, not just public health busybodies.

The CVM / CRM framework clearly only works with licit transactions and activity – orchestrated by responsible actors and willing consumers – but there are otherwise few limits to it.

It doesn't need to be restricted simply to psychoactive substances either. The inclusion of ordinary prescription and "Over the Counter" (OTC) medications could have significant value. Elsewhere in the healthcare sector, insurers have already encouraged the take-up of fitness tracker watches and devices, and the sharing of ultra-personal data for mutual benefits – if you keep moving, discounts apply.[111]

The opportunity for software-led pharma-related services is on an altogether different scale. The chemical interaction of alcohol with many pharmaceutical products raises personal risk levels substantially, a relationship that is not well understood by ordinary consumers.[112] Tools to help alleviate this risk could address and improve fatality rates.

The legitimate pharmaceutical industry is also plagued by three other issues that could benefit from customer-centric data services: the (non-)adherence[113] of patients/customers to prescribed consumption recommendations,[114] the diversion of prescribed medicines to non-patients, and the growing problem of counterfeit substances entering supply-chains. Improving medication adherence alone represents many billions of dollars-worth of prospective value,[115] even if gains are only gradual.

Prescription-monitoring systems have been introduced by some regulators to try and control supply, for example by preventing over-prescription of opioid drugs by physicians.[116] In most markets, including the most commercially valuable, these systems are in their infancy. Meanwhile, there is little innovation in ensuring compliance with courses of valuable medicines and the appropriate disposal of surplus drugs.

The problem of counterfeit pharmaceuticals is not new in emerging markets,[117] and is now spreading to the supply-chains of more developed countries, despite best efforts. Printing and packaging technologies, among others, make the creation of fakes easier than ever. A counterfeit drug may be ineffective, inert, or worse. If you are expecting a name-brand drug to treat your epilepsy or heart disease, the consequences of inadvertently taking a fake could be devastating.[118]

Patients are obviously the greatest losers from the practice but the global pharmaceutical industry has much to gain if counterfeiting can be successfully countered by adopting new customer-centric technologies.[119]

Commercial pharma-related offerings could easily bubble up from start-ups and others in a sector that is accustomed to massive-scale research and development. Fast-growing, comparatively predictable revenue streams from new value-added services that address long-standing problems would be welcomed by industry investors. Across all industries, it will be key to maintain consumer confidence in all of the potential civil liberty and data governance issues concerned, what we can loosely term privacy.

Fortunately, there is precedent for the kind of ecosystem that we need to build out. The basic building block is the comparatively simple point-of-sale reward scheme, such as those long operated by supermarkets the world over.[120] A more complex model is that of the coalition reward scheme, where multiple trading entities pool their data, with the unique customer as the common linkage.[121]

The most well-known of coalition schemes are travel-orientated, linking airlines with partners such as credit card providers or operators of independent schemes like fuel providers or supermarkets.[122] The coalition operator creates value by combining the data sourced from partners into valuable new customer-level information – knowledge that would not otherwise exist.

Designing a narcotech ecosystem that works or can be adapted globally is not a simple undertaking. Regulations that already vary by country or region may be outpaced by technical or social developments.

The potential for bad actors needs to be considered too, at every level. Design for utopia but be mindful of dystopia. Features that may seem helpful one day can come to be regretted subsequently. Governments and political leaders come and go, be they authoritarian or classically liberal in outlook, democratic or otherwise. Corporate behavior can also frequently disappoint, even if it is explicitly prohibited or subsequently attributed to unforeseen weaknesses.

Data integrity and security are of the utmost concern. The experience consumers have had with social media and other companies will challenge the adoption and viability of otherwise desirable services. At the same time, we would be unwise to await an arm of government, national or otherwise, to request or legislate a suitable solution. We might be waiting forever.

Instead, we are going to have to do it ourselves.

Five key points

- Consumer-centric information will help ordinary citizens and other stakeholders make better quality decisions

- A multitude of ecosystems and service-providers will monetize raw, ultra-personal data

- A single-customer view is critical – it provides the link for combining and creating new information from basic raw data

- Existing consumer reward schemes illustrate the principal

- Trust in service-providers and privacy concerns are paramount

Innovation the Narcotech way

- The path to change from a practical perspective

There is a wealth of technology talent across the world, ranging from gifted individuals to large, highly competent teams. It is predominantly, but not exclusively, found in the private sector. Adept at finding solutions to challenges, when motivated and incentivized such talents can move the proverbial mountains that otherwise impede progress.

Government institutions the world over have an appalling track record in IT systems development and procurement. Many would say that this also applies to the regulatory systems they devise and oversee, but smart regulation can and does exist – it is simply rarer than desirable.

In the context of permitting the development of licit substance narcotech ecosystems, the role of the state should, in as many instances as possible, be as an enabler of bottom-up iterative development rather than a top-down prescriber.

Intervention by governments in the actual design and framework of solutions is best limited to instances of outright market failure or those areas where only legislation can compel the delivery of needed consumer benefits. An example of this would be when a producer or supplier of a licit substance refuses to participate in a previously anticipated manner.

Innovative hardware technologies, such as new forms of sensors or measuring devices, will typically be patentable designs whose commercial rights can be protected by established laws covering designs and other intellectual property. In the context of narcotech, there are likely significant opportunities to profit from developing physical devices and linking them to specific consumers. But the most valuable opportunities will be in the creation of software and tools that exploit and link all of the newly available data, not just that which is device-related.

There won't be a single ecosystem but an ever-expanding and adapting range of interlocking ecosystems, all centered around the individual consumer – whether their identity is exposed to an end-use application or not.

The open-source software movement[123] presents the model for deploying the skills and intellectual firepower needed to quickly and successfully make the software-related gains required. This is the same methodology that enables ongoing improvement and customization of the Linux computer operating system. Linux in its various manifestations underpins much of the Internet and enterprise IT infrastructure in use today.[124]

Rather than Intellectual Property rights being controlled by a single proprietary software developer, an open-source framework can enable the widest and most capable range of talents to collectively design and build out systems at speed – optimizing and remedying shortcomings as they go.

By democratizing and decentralizing development and customization, commercial ownership rights are likewise distributed – helping address monopolistic concerns before government intervention is necessary.

Critically, open-sourcing can stimulate diffuse partners to rapidly collaborate, integrate, and scale. These are the qualities needed to maximize potential outcomes within the shortest possible timeframes.

Instigating and co-ordinating the growth of narcotech hardware and software opportunities will be a disparate range of service-providers, creating and utilizing other forms of intellectual property. Measured by a kaleidoscopic range of performance indicators, these actors may be in the private sector, public sector, or be non-profits.

The full social value of their contributions will be more challenging to measure than simply tallying their revenues, but it is in this role that they could be most influential. If an initiative is thought to decrease the incidence of a harmful activity, what monetary value do we place on the harm prevented? Specialist health economists have techniques to attempt to answer this and other questions, but they need good quality raw materials, data, to work with.

Narcotech provides them that.

Quality also needs addressing, in several different guises. There is a need to maximize consumer confidence that their privacy interests are being protected; that a technology, be it data content-created or a technical application, is what is claimed.

A typical way to address this might be via industry bodies, certifications, and recognized standards but at present there is no industry to speak of, no commonality of interest, and little to no funding or profit-incentive to encourage co-operation. It is the classic chicken-and-egg problem: which comes first.

The interim solution is to rely on branding narcotech itself, attempting where possible to open-source and democratize ownership, providing incentives towards establishing and policing common standards.

A brand is far more than a recognizable logo or registered trademark. It can be trusted and its values universally understood. In the case of narcotech, it encompasses all the privacy and minority–majority protections that could arise, the consumer-centric values that aim for positive social outcomes.

Narcotech should be the measure by which any design iteration or new service, irrespective of complexity, is assessed as fit-for-purpose. This applies whether it is merely a simple new feature or enabling an entirely new commercial use case.

In the next chapter we will look at how to make a fast start with nicotine products and cannabis.

Five key points

- Narcotech offers the promise of creating new value for consumers and other stakeholders, focused on personal health

- There are opportunities for both hardware and software technologies to be developed

- The open-source model offers the best mix of speed, co-operation and distribution of effort

- The licensed user concept can be adapted according to circumstances

- Narcotech is an umbrella term encompassing desirable traits such as quality and privacy

Part 4: Moving Forwards Fast

Tobacco and nicotine

- Demonstrating success with smoke signals

The concept of narcotech is ready to go live today, irrespective of the status of illicit drug reform. Indeed, the speed of drug reform could be accelerated if successes are demonstrated with troublesome substances that are licit today.

The obvious first candidate is nicotine. Not just combustible tobacco but the whole range of nicotine delivery systems that have mushroomed in many markets – notably e-cigarettes and vapes, but also alternative tobacco products such as heated tobacco and medical substitutes like nicotine chewing gum. Synthetic nicotine, made in laboratories rather than grown in plantations, would also be in scope. (Full disclosure: your author smoked tobacco – with attempts to stop – from his early teens to his early forties. He has now successfully stopped for more than a decade, aided by gum.)

Despite its longstanding revenue-raising record, the tobacco industry and its dependent customers have few friends either in governments or the general population. The arguments about the merits or otherwise of tobacco smoking have long been settled, and both smokers and the industry are minorities vulnerable to being 'bullied' by majorities, notwithstanding their tax contributions.[125]

The bullish would say that as there are over 190 nation states in the United Nations, the testing of voluntary personal licensing and forced industry co-operation should be easily achievable somewhere in the world, commencing sooner rather than later.

Many aggrieved or fanatical citizens might wish that licensing was involuntary or smoking entirely prohibited, scenarios with which this publication and the philosophy of narcotech disagree. It is, however, testament to the influence of the tobacco lobby worldwide that in recent history, only the tiny state of Bhutan has actually attempted the outright prohibition of all tobacco smoking. [126]

There are other valid reasons to take care over testing voluntary, rather than mandatory, personal licensing: tobacco has nearly as long a history of smuggling, tax avoidance, misrepresentation, and other forms of deviance as the history of smoking itself. Minimizing the extent and influence of black and grey market activity is imperative. In many territories, gangsters and their like see tobacco as a lucrative commodity attracting less severe penalties than 'normal' illicit drugs when sold as contraband. [127]

Success will rely on building and maintaining a high participation rate by all concerned parties, centered on the consensual agreement to public policies and controls in force. Fundamental to this is compliance with and adherence to all relevant taxation and regulatory regimes.

While careful development and implementation can mitigate and minimize deviation risks, the opportunity for and extent of transgression will be determined by three factors: the prevailing levels of taxation; the legitimacy of ongoing law enforcement activities; gaining the consent of consumers to the collection and use of their personal data.

Narcotech's principal contribution is to the third of these, establishing the framework to maximize voluntary participation and co-operation by smokers themselves. Otherwise, the very concept of consent could easily overwhelm or else be simply ignored by indifferent individuals. Loved-ones can play a role through encouragement of participation. Additionally, it is recommended that consumers can flexibly delegate responsibility to one or more third-party service-providers acting on their behalf, such as the membership-based communities discussed in Part Two.

So where to begin?

Your author is British and resident in the UK, so naturally looks to the UK environment as suitable for testing reform with tobacco and nicotine. There are also strong reasons for choosing the UK.

The UK has well established legal and commercial systems, a decent technology skills base, and the relative independence of not being part of either a larger trading block or complex federated system of regulations such as in the USA or the European Union. The UK also has, for better or worse, the National Health Service (NHS), in practice a near-monopoly state-provider of health care services.[128]

The existence of the NHS, unlike more fragmented systems in other countries, means that its centralization of policy[129] and health records[130] could provide useful leverage, at the very least in regard to research and analysis. It is also making progress with digitization, with some services available via a nationally standardized mobile phone app.[131]

The UK is also a world-leader in the prevalence of e-cigarette and electronic vaping usage, with over three million adult users.[132] Compared to many nations around the world, the UK has a liberal approach to the sale and distribution of electronic drug delivery systems,[133] many of which are or could become network-capable.

Critically, the retailing environment for tobacco, e-cigarette, and pharmacy-type medications is highly regulated already,[134] yet flexible enough to adapt if needed to new point-of-sale technologies. In virtually all instances, retailers are capable of connecting to computer networks, while the basic principles of supermarket reward scheme technologies are already well comprehended by consumers.

So how does it get started?

People power is important – politicians and regulators do respond to lobbying, if its demands are focused and can be applied. The greatest beneficiaries of improving outcomes are smokers themselves. Self-interest in new and novel services should be a powerful motivator to back organizations or others acting on their behalf. Smokers will also be interested in protecting their civil liberties.

Nascent narcotech service-providers may be able to see profit opportunities in driving forward development. The direct commercial opportunity is a base of about six million adult smokers and three million adult vapers, with substantial overlap.[135] Virtually all of these consumers have concerned family members, plus there are massive constituencies of strong opinion-holders within the ranks of non-smokers, ex-smokers, and the countless millions who have seen friends and family suffer smoking-related harm.

Your author expects to get the ball rolling in the UK with a membership-based news and analysis service, to be followed by further services in time.

Five key points

- Narcotech can step-change the regulation and outcomes of inherently risky behavior

- Success with existing legal substances can path-find towards making the illicit legally available

- Nicotine – combustible, vaped or otherwise – is an obvious candidate for experimenting with the licensed user concept

- The UK's unique characteristics makes it the ideal test environment for new nicotine controls and to evaluate outcomes

- Resistance can be expected from some stakeholders but can

be mitigated by careful design and consensus-building

The special case of alcohol

- Why narcotech needs to be flexible and have consumer buy-in

Alcohol is a special case.

Despite most definitely being an intoxicating substance, most societies around the world are reluctant to treat it as a drug *per se*, instead qualifying it as something apart. In English, the terminology is routinely "drugs and alcohol".

The importance of local culture cannot be overstated. The social acceptability of heavy drinking in Russia[136] and Japan[137] is vastly different with, say, the expectation of comparatively modest consumption among most Italians.

Alcohol has played a fundamental and often sacred role in the development of most civilizations for millennia. Social rituals are deeply engrained and usage consequences well understood, good and bad. The status quo is largely accepted. This is to the great frustration of the intolerant who believe that ethanol – the chemical name for the drinkable form of alcohol – is to all intents and purposes a drug, and an especially dangerous one at that.

The numbers of people who think that they have suffered harms from the consequences of alcohol consumption are substantial. Compounding the issue is the fact that often the harms befall innocent individuals due to the consumption behavior of others. The list of potential harms is extensive and varied: liver damage, susceptibility to cancers, violence, harm to the unborn, family breakdown, drink-driving, social nuisance, and so on.

Given the sheer variety, sophistication, and size of the existing consumption markets, there is huge scope for new technology-based initiatives to attempt to prevent some of these harms.

For most drinkers, unless they experience serious consequences – and even if they do – alcohol consumption is a life-long pastime, even if consumption patterns change with life stages. The greatest potential for narcotech is in successfully addressing issues earlier in a consumer's drinking career, remedying behaviors and realizing benefits before costs to the individual and society escalate and accumulate over time. This is strongly in the long-term interests of both consumers and producers. Alcoholism is a complex condition that does not develop overnight.

Consumer participation in narcotech technologies should be stimulated by benefits rather than penalties, which means voluntary rather than mandatory participation. Legitimate exceptions to the 'only voluntary' principle might include violent offenders being dealt with by the criminal justice system.

Many societies and social grouping strongly discourage the distribution and consumption of alcoholic drinks, with some banning it outright, in a similar manner to illicit drug prohibition. With laws established nationally rather than internationally, the results have been varied.

Throughout the Muslim world, alcohol is treated as forbidden for adherents. In some Muslim countries, restrictions apply not only to Muslim citizens, but to all citizens and visitors too.[138] Compliance with such laws is high but not universal – and freedom of choice for the individual is greatly curtailed. Meanwhile, Scandinavian countries tax and regulate the sale of alcohol much more strictly than their counterparts in Southern Europe.[139] Their leaders feel that in the absence of such restrictions, there would be greater drunkenness resulting in assorted harms.

In Australia, alcohol was introduced to indigenous peoples during the period of colonization that started from 1770. Subsequently, laws and draconian policies have been repeatedly introduced and withdrawn by government bodies attempting to control the sale and purchase of alcohol specifically by Aboriginal and Torres Strait Islander communities.[140] Even today, many rural communities are subject to locality-specific restrictions aimed at alleviating social harms arising from excessive consumption.[141] Success has always been limited, complicated by socio-economic factors.

Worldwide, there is a long history of governments applying taxes to the production and consumption of alcohol, to generate revenues and to influence behaviors. Typically, higher strength products, such as spirits, attract proportionately higher rates of tax than less potent drinks. In many less well-off societies, the levels of taxation are unaffordable for the poor and the illicit production of untaxed moonshine products is rife (for example, the home-brewed spirit *changaa* in Kenya).[142] Poor production techniques mean that methanol poisoning, which can cause blindness and even death, is the occasional consequence for an unfortunate few.[143]

For the majority of consumers worldwide, the overall pleasures from alcohol consumption significantly outweigh the negatives, even when alcohol is drunk to excess and the outcomes are poor. That is not to downplay the negatives, but to recognize that alcohol enjoys a unique status among the ranks of psychoactive substances because of the history, maturity and complexity of its role in society.

Because of the sheer scale of the global customer base and the pre-existing social acceptability of alcohol in the wealthiest consumer markets (even if not with all regulators), narcotech has massive commercial potential that could be realized quite quickly by the likes of independent software developers and other innovators.

Only poor regulation can mess it up. Undue interference with long-standing personal freedoms would be a fast-track to losing popular respect, legitimacy, and, consequently, participation.

Five key points

- Alcohol is a psychoactive substance whose consumers can benefit from applied personal health technologies

- Alcohol regulatory systems vary widely around the world, from the most liberal to the tightly monitored

- The maturity and complexity of the sector presents a wide range of opportunities and challenges

- Participation will typically be voluntary, stimulated by benefits not penalties

- The assessment of risk, such as interactions with pharmaceutical products, is a key development area for service-providers

Cannabis

- Reining in the excesses of liberalization

The political will to substantially amend international drug conventions and treaties is simply not there at present. Given the conservative nature of the decision-makers and the processes at the relevant institutions, it is hard to see significant reforms emerging via diplomatic consensus.

Rather more likely is that the conventions will gradually be ignored and circumvented by more powerful states acting as first movers,[144] swiftly copied by others.[145] The current arrangements will fade into obscurity, to be superseded by updated practices. This will take a protracted period, probably over a decade, possibly longer.

Already, those countries that are experimenting with cannabis reforms are acting unilaterally, in contravention of the norms of international relations.[146] They attempt where possible to comply with treaty obligations but the restrictions are no longer seen to be quite as sacrosanct as they once were.

Although in most territories there are no planned moves to make currently illicit substances licit, the appetite for this could change rapidly. There are many keen observers of the cannabis experimenters, not least in long-suffering coca-leaf producer countries.[147] In the EU, Germany will set the pace for change, though the execution of proposed plans are vulnerable to delay if other member states interfere via the mechanism of the European Commission.[148]

Although there are serious teething issues, the North American cannabis liberalization experience has not led to the disastrous consequences anticipated by skeptics. Its relative success to date means that rollback is increasingly unlikely. If and when the USA chooses to enact federal re-regulation of cannabis, the global pace of change will accelerate too.

The chemical make-up of the cannabis plant is exceedingly complex. Alongside the intoxicating chemical THC, responsible for the recreational high, the plant generates dozens of other compounds that are non-intoxicating, including the well-known cannabinoid, CBD. This substance is now widely marketed in several countries in a variety of wellness products, which are now attracting regulatory interest themselves.[149]

The medicalization of cannabis greatly complicates the regulation of recreational cannabis everywhere, regardless of locally prevailing laws. Research into cannabis has exploded internationally in the last two decades as medical research licensing has undergone some liberalization. In the USA, however, scheduling restrictions continue to hamper medical research despite the rapidly evolving federal regulatory landscape.[150] A veritable 'green rush' of investors seek to understand and commercialize novel treatments for a huge number of ailments.[151]

The established pharmaceutical industry, which focuses on isolating specific compounds and proving medical benefits using long-established methods, has found the complexity and politicization of cannabis challenging.[152] Consumer advocates for medical cannabis are vocal and much of the science is new and uncertain. The strategy of drug law reformers to use medical access as a precursor to recreational access has heightened confusion about the potential capabilities of cannabis-derived products.[153]

In the USA, parts of the medical profession have discredited themselves over the lax granting of access to medical cannabis cards in states where recreational use has been illegal at the time.[154] Even where adult recreational use sales are legal, North American retailers – who style themselves as dispensaries – are essentially supplying identical products to both types of customers, with differential tax rates applying.[155]

Medical patient users, by virtue of their needs, may be amongst the heaviest regular consumers of intoxicating produce, leading skeptics to liken medical dispensation as being akin to a discount card for substance abusers.[156] The medical–recreational dual nature of cannabis lends itself strongly to personal licensing in those countries and regions where either purpose is licit. Beyond practicalities such as determining the position of international travelers and their medications,[157] there are strong social reasons to push for personal licensing, voluntary or otherwise.

These include, for instance, discouraging nuisance public consumption, ensuring that products have been obtained through legitimate channels with applicable taxes levied, and reducing the risk of diversion to minors.

There is considerable scientific debate about the risks of serious psychiatric illnesses either being caused or exacerbated by the use of cannabis products, whether consumed for medical purposes or otherwise.[158] Episodes of psychosis, though comparatively rare, are typically life-changing experiences and extremely costly to treat. Younger populations are thought to be most vulnerable. Personal licensing and mental health insurance requirements would go some way towards mitigating these risks for individuals and wider society.

Such social reasons are a good illustration of how a non-consuming majority can consensually steer the behavior of a minority, when a product is licit. Different societies will adopt different approaches to enforcement but even the most irresponsible of consumers can understand the reasoning that they have responsibilities towards broader society, not just freedom of personal choice.

If a consumer wishes to be protected both by and from the state, they correspondingly have the responsibility to protect the state system. They can only do this by choosing wisely and consensually adhering to the regulatory regime.

There is a balance to be struck. Otherwise, we are back to the status quo.

Five key points

- The legal availability of cannabis is posing challenges to regulatory bodies

- There has been a focus on liberalizing supply, with few obligations on consumers

- Narcotech has the potential to demonstrate how technologies can alleviate harms

- Personal licensing can assist in discovering and pricing the real levels of risk

- Policy successes will be copied in new territories and other substance categories

Conclusion

- What might a decade's progress result in

No one sets out in life to become dependent on something that harms them. Likewise, no society seeks to burden itself with health, social and security costs that unnecessarily lower living standards and quality of life, while holding back the pace of productivity growth and socio-economic development.

Those individuals that find themselves dependent can be motivated to help themselves, given the right conditions and assistance. Yet for too long, resources have been wasted in futile and destructive attempts to work against human nature, rather than with it.

Narcotech technology and service innovations raise the prospect of individuals and societies improving their quality of life, if the will is there to allow them to develop and flourish. Narcotech-type personal surveillance technologies are inevitable over the long run, but it is critical that their application is steered by ordinary citizens so that existing freedoms are respected. This responsibility lies with-individual consumers and their political representatives, as much as with the technocrats and software developers who will frame regulations and design apps that utilize rich new data streams. Better that than the dystopian prospect of technologies being developed for an untouchable state and its partners, applied coercively.

We live in a time when exponential improvements in computer processing power allow for explosive growth in human knowledge.

There is the possibility of a chance transformative breakthrough which suddenly upends our understanding of psychoactive substances and human consciousness. Such an eventuality falls into what former US Defense Secretary Donald Rumsfeld famously described as "unknown unknowns".[159]

Such a scientific discovery might arise from applying Artificial Intelligence algorithms to the renewed research into psychedelics, attempts to link computers and the human brain, or something entirely unanticipated. As the late baseball legend Yogi Berra reputedly said, "It's tough to make predictions, especially about the future." Nevertheless, it is possible to forecast some likely outcomes over the medium to long term.

The most transformative development in the medium term should be the introduction of personal licensing for tobacco and nicotine consumption. This could enjoy massive popular support and be adopted at speed despite push-back from producers and concerns about creating black markets. In most countries it can be expected to eventually become mandatory for combustible tobacco, helping consumption of which to decline even faster than currently. Civil liberty concerns will be assuaged by comparatively looser restrictions on other nicotine preparations.

Tobacco industry shareholders can be expected to suffer from effective narcotech as envisaged, though it should be noted that their demise has been predicted several times before. The tobacco industry itself is clear that combustible tobacco is in permanent decline, hence it's interest in substitute tobacco and nicotine products. However, it seems unlikely that the industry will be permitted to establish profit-earning capabilities equivalent to those enjoyed historically.

In parallel to successful tobacco smoking controls, regulators will likely model the legalization and re-regulation of cannabis – both medical and recreational – on a similar personal licensing basis to try and quash black market activity, which has persisted in Canada and those US states where cannabis can be obtained legally.[160]

In Canada, different states have experimented with differing approaches to retail store availability; in California, local zoning regulations and taxation-related issues have held back legal participation. Critically the licensed user model has not featured in either territory to date; controls have centered on the supply-chain.

In the medium term, it is unlikely that mainstream voters will tolerate ongoing mass law-breaking and tax evasion by cannabis consumers (and others), if legitimate products are available. Personal licensing, offers a compromise solution that places civic responsibility in the hands of the consumer.

Irrespective of the substance in question, personal licensing regulations and tax laws will require enforcement to be effective. This need not entail a return to the oppressive conditions prevailing under prohibition, but will require consumers to take personal responsibility, self-regulate and participate as full members of society. The alternative is a return to the situations of old, or worse.

Driven by concerns about tax revenue-leakage and continued criminality, enforcement efforts will likely enjoy renewed popular support: in the court of public opinion, tax avoidance is legitimate and acceptable, tax evasion is not. Personal licensing provides all parties with the mechanism to arrive at a mutually acceptable outcome.

When personal licensing can be seen to work effectively, voters, politicians and consumers will demand its applicability for other substances under consideration.

Other contexts will include medical prescription and the supervised dispensing of a limited range of other substances in bolder, wealthier jurisdictions. Vancouver, Canada is already piloting forms of 'safe supply' programs[161] and Dutch activists have mocked up how MDMA might be distributed non-medically[162]. Such developments will be accompanied by innovation in treatment strategies over the medium to long term, including displacing demand for the most harmful concoctions with less potent legal substitutes. Mild coca products in particular will be a commercial and social success once widely available.

As discussed in the previous chapter, alcohol is a special case and can be expected to have the most complex range of developments. Globally, the producers and retailers of alcoholic drinks should thrive with narcotech, despite possible fears from the industry itself. The size of the existing base of alcohol consumers is at little risk of significant shrinkage unless there is radical change in demand due to the legalization of other intoxicants, and the combination of population and economic growth in emerging economies, plus increasing secularism, will continue to boost their total addressable markets.

In mature democracies with older populations and long-established cultural acceptability of alcohol, the opportunity for industry to add value to existing products and services should stimulate voluntary engagement levels, while current trends suggesting growing interest in personal health will help drive consumer adoption.

In countries with younger populations or more autocratic styles of governance, formal alcohol regulations may be strengthened with the aid of narcotech-style solutions. This may be particularly so in countries experiencing rapid socio-economic change and digitization in everyday life. In the Arab and Muslim-majority world, the actual availability of alcohol may be liberalized for those that wish to access it, beyond, for example, the existing systems applicable to foreigners in Qatar[163] and predicted for special zones in Saudi Arabia.[164]

Where things may get particularly interesting – and valuable – is where there is meaningful progress in helping consumers better understand adverse interactions between alcohol and pharmaceutical medications. Given the legality of all input factors, there is no reason not to anticipate significant, potentially lifesaving, developments in the short to medium term led by the health care sector.

As befits an industry that broadly specializes in research and the high-quality manufacture of chemical compounds, the pharmaceutical sector in general should do well from global drug reform, albeit moving ahead cautiously at first. New intellectual property will take time to identify, patent, and to generate commercial returns; faster progress may be made on new service developments related to existing non-psychoactive medications.

Reduced counterfeiting and increased prescription-adherence could be within reach in the short-term, benefiting traditional pharma companies large and small, and broader society too. Further ahead, rather than the "Big Pharma" organizations that activists are wary of today, it will be new entrants or spin-outs that take on the production and supervision responsibilities for more leisure-orientated products and services.

The biggest losers from the success of narcotech will be those whose livelihoods and profits depend on the illegal supply of drugs. As societies feel confident enough to legalize and make the illicit licit, we can realistically hope that black market activity will reduce and illegal profits shrink.

Despite glamorization of their activities in the media, illegal drug traffickers and dealers are not popular characters in the public imagination; even their best clients tend only to respect them for practical reasons. Few will cry for them if they suffer revenue-loss or, for that matter, fade into oblivion.

There will be more sympathy for growers and low-level workers, especially in the types of remote regions where there are few other commercial opportunities. Coca-growing regions in South America fall into this category, as do illegal opium growers around the world.

Even where their produce becomes licit, for instance coca tea and the like, other non-traditional producers may out-compete them when breaking laws is no longer a production requirement. These may be farmers who are better able to scale and automate, perhaps in countries we don't currently associate with particular crops but which are more than capable of producing them.[165]

Organized crime groups involved in drugs will continue to prosper while black market profits are available. If opportunities fade in specific markets or for specific products, they will switch their attention to new areas and types of crime – unfortunately, it is an industry which continually evolves according to circumstances.

More likely, drug cartels, mafias, and gangs – and they are all merely opportunistic, entrepreneurial gangs at heart – will simply wither away over time if they no longer enjoy extraordinary profits in particular markets. Legal changes will undoubtedly be relatively slow and progress to reform well signposted. Even the most sophisticated criminals today are not drawing up detailed business plans for long periods. Money-launderers and other parasitic support industries may see a reduction in business volumes following successful drug reform. They always have the option to seek fresh customer segments.

In countries with weaker legal systems and especially violent histories, there may be well-funded calls for the forgiveness of drug-related crimes. In the USA, interest groups have already successfully sought the expungement of historic drug convictions for some non-violent offenders.[166]

On the legitimate side of crime, adjustment among the forces of law and order will be slow, gradual, and relatively minor. Campaigners would be completely wrong to expect policing numbers and costs to fall. Far from it. New and amended drug laws will still need applying, on a more consensual basis. Indeed, new laws and regulations can likely be enforced more effectively than existing ones, once levels of corruption and law-breaking become less normalized than at present.

Criminologists and penal reformers will hope to reduce the influence of the prison–industrial complex in some countries, having attributed much of its growth to drug prohibition regimes.[167] There are significant vested interests here, not limited to unions and prisons constructed to support high incarceration rates. They can be expected to seek new clients if the volumes of drug-related offenders fall. Especially in places where penal institutions have become private or semi-private businesses. A radical rethink of incarceration policy in general may be warranted.

The deployment of narcotech technologies should expand personal choice and freedom, while steering consumers towards less harmful and reckless behavior, helping to bring addictions to an end. Reductions in crime and increases in tax revenue will benefit governments, whose researchers will have better quality data with which to devise policies. Technology developments can raise employment rates, skills, and workforce productivity. Entirely new categories of knowledge and industry should develop, with shareholders who take legitimate risks rewarded with profit.

Profit is not a dirty word. In the Introduction to this book, two types of profit are described. One is financial, allowing accurate measurement of results. The other is social benefit, an intangible that is much more challenging to quantify. The objective of narcotech is to achieve both of these.

Real innovation opportunities abound with narcotech, whether they are executed by tiny start-ups or spun out of the operations of established corporations. Financiers, whether from venture capital, private equity, or banking institutions, are always seeking new investments of merit.

They will be spoilt for choice. The world's legitimate entrepreneurs and businesspeople simply need to be set free to do their thing.

Five key points

- Personal licensing for nicotine products is inevitable

- The alcohol and pharma industries will create the most narcotech value

- Surveillance technologies are unstoppable and will multiply

- There will be privacy battles to control personal information

- Drug-related criminality will fade away slowly over time

Endnotes

---

[1] Fact sheets: tobacco, World Health Organisation, 24.05.2022 (https://www.who.int/news-room/fact-sheets/detail/tobacco).

[2] Global status report on alcohol and health 2018, World Health Organisation, 18.10.2018 (https://www.who.int/publications/i/item/a-summary-of-the-global-status-report-on-alcohol).

[3] World Drug Report 2022, United Nations Office on Drugs and Crime, 27.06.2022 (https://www.unodc.org/unodc/en/data-and-analysis/world-drug-report-2022.html).

[4] Average Cost of Drug Rehab, National Centre for Drug Abuse Statistics, 29.09.2022 (https://drugabusestatistics.org/cost-of-rehab/).

[5] Treaties, United Nations Office on Drugs and Crime, 29.09.2022 (https://www.unodc.org/unodc/en/treaties/index.html).

[6] Sacklers to pay $6 billion to settle Purdue opioid lawsuits, Reuters, 04.03.2022 (https://www.reuters.com/business/healthcare-pharmaceuticals/sacklers-will-pay-up-6-bln-resolve-purdue-opioid-lawsuits-mediator-2022-03-03/).

[7] The War on Alcohol; Lisa McGirr, W.W. Norton and Company, 29.11.2016 (https://wwnorton.com/books/The-War-on-Alcohol/).

[8] Peter Reuter, Jonathan P. Caulkins & Greg Midgette, Heroin use cannot be measured adequately with a general population survey, Society for the Study of Addiction, October 2021 (https://pubmed.ncbi.nlm.nih.gov/33651441/).

[9] Kai Strittmatter, We Have Been Harmonised, Old Street Publishing, 29.09.2022 (https://www.amazon.com/We-Have-Been-Harmonized-Surveillance/dp/0063027305/).

[10] Helen Clark, Opioid shortages open up a world of pain, Financial Times, 29.06.2020 (https://www.ft.com/content/97c51a2a-e600-402e-9015-95d3ba32ab05).

[11] Topic page, Vice.com, 29.09.2022 (https://www.vice.com/en/topic/encrochat).

[12] Max Daly, Synthetic Drugs Will Change the Global Drug Trade Forever, Vice.com, 24.05.2022 (https://www.vice.com/en/article/gyzx57/synthetic-drugs-could-change-the-global-drug-trade-forever-v26n3).

[13] Teens On Instagram Can Still Easily Access Illegal Drugs, New Research Shows, Forbes.com, 17.05.2022 (https://www.forbes.com/sites/abrambrown/2022/05/17/teens-on-instagram-can-still-easily-access-illegal-drugs-new-research-shows/).

[14] dataUNODC, United Nations Office on Drugs and Crime, 29.09.2022 (https://dataunodc.un.org/dp-drug-prices-Europe-USA).

[15] Mo Constandi, A brief history of psychedelic psychiatry, The Guardian, 02.09.2014 (https://www.theguardian.com/science/neurophilosophy/2014/sep/02/psychedelic-psychiatry).

[16] Jo Neil, Tripping over red tape: psychedelics for mental health, Drug Science, 07.03.2022 (https://www.drugscience.org.uk/psychedelic-research-for-mental-health-uk/).

[17] Rachel Roubein, Biden's directive on marijuana faces a Catch-22, The Washington Post, 10.10.2022 (https://www.washingtonpost.com/politics/2022/10/10/biden-directive-marijuana-faces-catch-22/)

[18] Psychoactive Substances Act 2016, UK Government, (https://www.gov.uk/government/collections/psychoactive-substances-bill-2015).

[19] Manisha Krishnan, The Future of Drugs Is a Synthetic Cocktail From Hell, Vice.com, 24.05.2022 (https://www.vice.com/en/article/g5qzpm/benzo-dope-tranq-future-of-overdose-crisis).

[20] Long, Jean (2010) Adulterants, bulking agents and contaminants in illicit drugs. Drugnet Ireland, Issue 35, Autumn 2010, pp. 18-20, HRB National Drugs Library, (https://www.drugsandalcohol.ie/13973/).

[21] Imperial College, London, (https://www.imperial.ac.uk/news/196673/new-wave-psychedelic-research-yielding-exciting/).

[22] Michael Eisenstein, The psychedelic escape from depression, Nature, 28.09.2022 (https://www.nature.com/articles/d41586-022-02872-9).

[23] Mandy Oaklander, Inside Ibogaine, One of the Most Promising and Perilous Psychedelics for Addiction, Time, 05.04.2021 (https://time.com/5951772/ibogaine-drug-treatment-addiction/).

[24] Dana Talesnik, McCurdy Studies Whether Kratom Can Reduce Opioid Withdrawal, Ease Pain, NIH Record, 24.06.2022 (https://nihrecord.nih.gov/2022/06/24/mccurdy-studies-whether-kratom-can-reduce-opioid-withdrawal-ease-pain).

[25] Frequently Asked Questions, American Psychiatric Association, 29.09.2022 (https://psychiatry.org/psychiatrists/practice/dsm/frequently-asked-questions).

[26] Keith Humphrey, Overcoming opioid regulation discord to put patients first, Stanford Medicine, 10.08.2022 (https://stanmed.stanford.edu/2022Issue1/opioid-crisis-consensus-prioritize-patients.html).

[27] Ethan Nadelmann, Twitter, 04.08.2022 (https://twitter.com/ethannadelmann/status/1554994473653919744).

[28] Maia Szalavitz, Undoing Drugs: How Harm Reduction Is Changing the Future of Drugs and Addiction, Hatchette Books, 27.07.2021 (https://www.hachettego.com/titles/maia-szalavitz/undoing-drugs/9780738285757/).

[29] Jan Hoffman, Fentanyl Test Strips Highlight Rift in Nation's Struggle to Combat Drug Deaths, New York Times, 01.10.2022 (https://www.nytimes.com/2022/10/01/health/fantanyl-test-strips.html).

[30] Drug Policy Alliance, (https://drugpolicy.org/issues/harm-reduction).

[31] Pioneering Middlesbrough heroin addiction clinic to close, BBC, 29.09.2022 (https://www.bbc.co.uk/news/uk-england-tees-63065334).

[32] How does The Loop's drug checking service work? , The Loop, 29.09.2022 (https://wearetheloop.org/about-drug-checking).

[33] Drug-Free Communities (DFC) Support Program, Office of National Drug Control Policy, 29.09.2022 (https://www.whitehouse.gov/

ondcp/dfc/).

[34] The Full Cost of the Opioid Crisis: $2.5 Trillion Over Four Years, Council of Economic Advisers, 28.10.2019 (https://trumpwhitehouse.archives.gov/articles/full-cost-opioid-crisis-2-5-trillion-four-years/).

[35] Trends and Statistics: Overdose Death Rates, National Institute on Drug Abuse, 29.09.2022 (https://nida.nih.gov/research-topics/trends-statistics/overdose-death-rates).

[36] World Health Organisation, 24.05.2022 (https://www.who.int/news-room/fact-sheets/detail/tobacco).

[37] Global status report on alcohol and health 2018, World Health Organisation, 09.05.2022 (https://www.who.int/publications/i/item/9789241565639).

[38] Global status report on alcohol and health 2018, World Health Organisation, 09.05.2022 (https://www.who.int/news-room/fact-sheets/detail/alcohol).

[39] Wastewater-based epidemiology and drugs topic page, European Monitoring Centre for Drugs and Drug Addiction, 29.09.2022 (https://www.emcdda.europa.eu/topics/wastewater_en).

[40] World Drug Report 2022, United Nations Office on Drugs and Crime, 27.06.2022 (https://www.unodc.org/unodc/en/data-and-analysis/world-drug-report-2022.html).

[41] Mexico's Long War: Drugs, Crime, and the Cartels, Council on Foreign Relations, 07.09.2022 (https://www.cfr.org/backgrounder/mexicos-long-war-drugs-crime-and-cartels).

[42] Mexico records deadliest year yet for journalists, with 18 murders so far -report, Reuters, 18.08.2022 (https://www.reuters.com/world/americas/mexico-records-deadliest-year-yet-journalists-with-18-murders-so-far-report-2022-08-18/).

[43] Police officer who stole drug dealers' cash jailed, BBC, 13.05.2021 (https://www.bbc.co.uk/news/uk-57100058).

[44] Tom Wainwright, Narconomics: How to Run a Drug Cartel, PublicAffairs, 23.02.2016 (https://www.amazon.com/Narconomics-How-Run-Drug-Cartel/dp/1610395832).

[45] Ayrshire man jailed after importing 250kg of cocaine bulking agent, National Crime Agency, 13.04.2022 (https://www.nationalcrimeagency.gov.uk/news/ayrshire-man-jailed-after-

importing-250kg-of-cocaine-bulking-agent).

[46] NHS worker jailed for taking 9g of cocaine into music festival on weekend off, The Mirror, 12.05.2022 (https://www.mirror.co.uk/news/uk-news/nhs-worker-jailed-taking-9g-26951514).

[47] Tony Romm, Democrats target cigarettes and vaping as potential sources to pay for $3.5 trillion economic package, Washington Post, 15.09.2021 (https://www.washingtonpost.com/us-policy/2021/09/15/congress-cigarettes-vaping-tax/).

[48] Where Smoking Breaks the Bank, statista, 28.09.2021 (https://www.statista.com/chart/15293/price-for-cigarettes-per-country/).

[49] Transnational illicit tobacco crime groups disrupted as part of global action on illicit tobacco trade, Australian Tax Office, 11.07.2022 (https://www.ato.gov.au/Media-centre/Media-releases/Transnational-illicit-tobacco-crime-groups-disrupted-as-part-of-global-action-on-illicit-tobacco-trade/).

[50] Colin Mendelson, Australia's Experiment With Prescription-Only Vapes Has Failed, Filter, 30.09.2022 (https://filtermag.org/australia-vape-prescriptions/).

[51] Andrea Figueras Ariso, Legal marijuana, but Uruguayans still prefer black market, Medical Xpress, 30.09.2022 (https://medicalxpress.com/news/2022-09-legal-marijuana-uruguayans-black.html).

[52] Ismail Sebuwaawo, Abu Dhabi Police stress need to fight drug abuse by providing treatment to addicts, Khaleej Times, 06.02.2022 (https://www.khaleejtimes.com/health/abu-dhabi-police-stress-need-to-fight-drug-abuse-by-providing-treatment-to-addicts).

[53] German Lopez, We have a solution for the opioid epidemic. It's dramatically underused., Vox, 17.12.2019 (https://www.vox.com/platform/amp/policy-and-politics/2019/12/17/18292021/opioid-epidemic-methadone-buprenorphine-naltrexone-drug-rehab).

[54] Professor Keith Humphreys, Twitter, 10.05.2021 (https://twitter.com/keithnhumphreys/status/1391741813677957120).

[55] Medications to Treat Opioid Use Disorder Research Report, National Institute on Drug Abuse, December 2021 (https://nida.nih.gov/publications/research-reports/medications-to-treat-opioid-addiction/efficacy-medications-opioid-use-disorder).

[56] Toby Seddon, Prescribing heroin: John Marks, the Merseyside clinics, and lessons from history, Internation Journal of Drug Policy,

April 2020 (https://pubmed.ncbi.nlm.nih.gov/32217353/).

[57] HEROIN ASSISTED TREATMENT Benefits and evidence to support its use, Transform Drug Policy Foundation, 30.09.2022 (https://transformdrugs.org/drug-policy/uk-drug-policy/heroin-assisted-treatment).

[58] Russell Newcombe, Twitter, 06.05.2021 (https://twitter.com/TheNewImpostor/status/1390391886955925506).

[59] Sam Quinones, The Least of Us: True Tales of America and Hope in the Time of Fentanyl and Meth, Bloomsbury Publishing, 02.11.2021 (https://www.amazon.com/Least-Us-Tales-America-Fentanyl/dp/1635574358/).

[60] Michael Shellenberger, San Fransicko: Why Progressives Ruin Cities, Harper, 12.10.2021 (https://www.amazon.com/San-Fransicko-Progressives-Ruin-Cities/dp/0063093626/).

[61] Strang, Lucy and Jirka Taylor, Heroin-Assisted Treatment and Supervised Drug Consumption Sites: Experience from Four Countries, Santa Monica, CA: RAND Corporation, December 2018 (https://www.rand.org/pubs/working_papers/WR1262.html).

[62] Addiction and mental health, BUPA, 30.09.2022 (https://www.bupa.co.uk/health/health-insurance/mental-health/support/addiction).

[63] Megan Leonhart, What you need to know about the cost and accessibility of mental health care in America, CNBC, 10.05.2021 (https://www.cnbc.com/2021/05/10/cost-and-accessibility-of-mental-health-care-in-america.html).

[64] Rehab Riviera, How some Southern California drug rehab centers exploit addiction, The Orange County Register, 21.05.2017 (https://www.ocregister.com/2017/05/21/how-some-southern-california-drug-rehab-centers-exploit-addiction/).

[65] German Lopez, The Rehab Racket: Investigating the high cost of addiction care, Vox, 06.09.2019 (https://www.vox.com/2019/9/6/20853284/drug-addiction-treatment-rehab-cost-vox).

[66] KING JAMES I, HIS COUNTERBLAST TO TOBACCO, 1604, Library of Virginia, 30.09.2022 (https://edu.lva.virginia.gov/dbva/items/show/124).

[67] Amos A, Haglund M. From social taboo to "torch of freedom": the marketing of cigarettes to women, Tobacco Control, 2000;9:3-8. (https://tobaccocontrol.bmj.com/content/9/1/3).

[68] The medieval beverage of choice: alcohol or water?, New Histories, 8, 2018-2019 (https://newhistories.group.shef.ac.uk/the-medieval-beverage-of-choice-alcohol-or-water/).

[69] History of Patent Medicine, Hagley Museum, 30.09.2022 (https://www.hagley.org/research/digital-exhibits/history-patent-medicine).

[70] Ella Lee, Fact check: Cocaine in Coke? Soda once contained drug but likely much less than post claims, USA Today, 25.07.2021 (https://eu.usatoday.com/story/news/factcheck/2021/07/25/fact-check-coke-once-contained-cocaine-but-likely-less-than-claimed/8008325002/).

[71] How to Regulate Stimulants 2020, p183, Transform Drug Policy Foundation, 30.09.2022 (https://transformdrugs.org/assets/files/PDFs/how-to-regulate-stimulants-full-text-medres-2020.pdf).

[72] Opium War, National Army Museum, 30.09.2022 (https://www.nam.ac.uk/explore/opium-war-1839-1842).

[73] The Opium Wars still shape China's view of the West, The Economist, 19.12.2017 (https://www.economist.com/christmas-specials/2017/12/19/the-opium-wars-still-shape-chinas-view-of-the-west).

[74] Samuel Hopkins Adams, The great American fraud : Articles on the nostrum evil and quacks, Collier's weekly, 1906 (https://wellcomecollection.org/works/rrx7d5jc).

[75] Barbara Berglund, Opium Dens in Chinatown, FoundSF, (https://www.foundsf.org/index.php?title=Opium_Dens_in_Chinatown).

[76] Larry Sloman, Reefer Madness: A History of Marijuana, , 15.11.1998 (https://www.amazon.com/Reefer-Madness-Larry-Ratso-Sloman/dp/0312195230).

[77] Carl L. Hart, How the Myth of the 'Negro Cocaine Fiend' Helped Shape American Drug Policy, The Nation, 29.01.2014 (https://www.thenation.com/article/archive/how-myth-negro-cocaine-fiend-helped-shape-american-drug-policy/).

[78] Pareto principle, Wikipedia, 30.09.2022 (https://en.wikipedia.org/wiki/Pareto_principle).

[79] J. Caulkins, Legalising Drugs Prudently: The Importance of Incentives and Values, Journal of Illicit Economies and Development,, 29.11.2019 (https://jied.lse.ac.uk/articles/10.31389/jied.44/).

[80] J. Caulkins, Legalising Drugs Prudently: The Importance of Incentives and Values, Journal of Illicit Economies and Development,, 29.11.2019 (https://jied.lse.ac.uk/articles/10.31389/jied.44/).

[81] E.J. Dionne, Jr. and Thomas E. Mann, Polling & Public Opinion: The good, the bad, and the ugly, The Brookings Institution, 01.05.2003 (https://www.brookings.edu/articles/polling-public-opinion-the-good-the-bad-and-the-ugly/).

[82] Ann Fordham, The war on drugs is built on racism. It's time to decolonise drug policies, International Drug Policy Consortium, 26.06.2020 (https://idpc.net/blog/2020/06/the-war-on-drugs-is-built-on-racism-it-s-time-to-decolonise-drug-policies).

[83] Kevin Sabet & Patrick J. Kennedy, Smokescreen: What the Marijuana Industry Doesn't Want You to Know, Forefront Books, 20.04.2021 (https://www.amazon.com/Smokescreen-What-Marijuana-Industry-Doesnt/dp/1948677873).

[84] Killings, robberies, extortion. California can't stop its booming illegal cannabis stores, The Los Angeles Times, 13.09.2022 (https://www.latimes.com/california/story/2022-09-13/illegal-weed-dispensaries-police-raids-crime).

[85] The war against money-laundering is being lost, The Economist, 12.04.2021 (https://www.economist.com/finance-and-economics/2021/04/12/the-war-against-money-laundering-is-being-lost).

[86] Home page, Global Commission on Drug Policy, 30.09.2022 (https://www.globalcommissionondrugs.org/).

[87] REGULATION - THE RESPONSIBLE CONTROL OF DRUGS, Global Commission on Drug Policy, 2018 (http://www.globalcommissionondrugs.org/reports/regulation-the-responsible-control-of-drugs).

[88] Jeffery C. Mays and Andy Newman, Nation's First Supervised Drug-Injection Sites Open in New York, New York Times, 30.11.2021 (https://www.nytimes.com/2021/11/30/nyregion/supervised-injection-sites-nyc.html).

[89] Phillip Oltermann, Germany's move to legalise cannabis slows over fears of clash with EU laws, The Guardian, 12.09.2022 (https://www.theguardian.com/world/2022/sep/12/germany-coalition-legalise-cannabis-laws-eu-european-court-justice).

[90] Independent Report: Making smoking obsolete, Javed Khan for UK

Government, 25.08.2022 (https://www.gov.uk/government/publications/the-khan-review-making-smoking-obsolete/making-smoking-obsolete-summary).

[91] Christopher Snowdon, Killjoys: A Critique of Paternalism, Institute of Economic Affairs, 10.11.2017 (https://iea.org.uk/publications/killjoys-a-critique-of-paternalism/).

[92] Department of Health, Targeting the European Commission: the seven lobbying techniques of Big Tobacco, University of Bath, 10.03.2021 (https://www.bath.ac.uk/announcements/targeting-the-european-commission-the-seven-lobbying-techniques-of-big-tobacco/).

[93] Leah Williams, Legalisation, Decriminalisation, and Prohibition, Drug Science, 21.01.2022 (https://www.drugscience.org.uk/drug-policy-explained-legalisation-decriminalisation-and-prohibition/).

[94] Missy Ryan, In test of ties with U.S., Colombian leader proposes shift on drugs, The Washington Post, 27.09.2022 (https://www.washingtonpost.com/national-security/2022/09/27/united-states-colombia-drugs/).

[95] Alan Philps interviewing President Juan Manuel Santos of Colombia, Chatham House, 01.08.2018 (https://www.chathamhouse.org/2012/08/president-juan-manuel-santos-colombia).

[96] Brian Winter, U.S.-led "war on drugs" questioned at U.N., Reuters, 26.09.2012 (https://www.reuters.com/article/us-un-assembly-mexico-drugs-idUSBRE88P1Q520120926).

[97] Drug Courts - Overview, US Department of Justice, 11.08.2020 (https://www.ojp.gov/feature/drug-courts/overview).

[98] New Zealand to ban cigarettes for future generations, BBC, 09.12.2021 (https://www.bbc.co.uk/news/world-asia-59589775).

[99] Home Office & Priti Patel MP, Illicit drug users to face tougher consequences, GOV.UK, 18.07.2022 (https://www.gov.uk/government/news/illicit-drug-users-to-face-tougher-consequences).

[100] Kai Strittmatter, We Have Been Harmonised, Old Street Publishing, 29.09.2022 (https://www.amazon.com/We-Have-Been-Harmonized-Surveillance/dp/0063027305/).

[101] Drew Donnelly, China Social Credit System Explained – What is it & How Does it Work?, Horizons, 22.09.2022 (https://

nhglobalpartners.com/china-social-credit-system-explained/).

[102] Cindy Yu, Mythbusting the social credit system, The Spectator, 13.06.2022 (https://www.spectator.co.uk/podcast/social-credit-system).

[103] Terms and Conditions - Alcohol and Tobacco, Nectar, 30.09.2022 (https://www.nectar.com/about/privacy-and-legal/i2c/cs-terms).

[104] Harm principle, Wikipedia, 01.10.2022 (https://en.wikipedia.org/wiki/Harm_principle).

[105] Coca tea, Wikipedia, 01.10.2022 (https://en.wikipedia.org/wiki/Coca_tea).

[106] Daniel Boffey, High street? Dutch ecstasy 'shop' shows possible way for drug reform, The Guardian, 18.08.2022 (https://www.theguardian.com/world/2022/aug/18/high-street-dutch-ecstasy-shop-shows-possible-way-for-drug-reform-xtc).

[107] Christina Majaski, What Is the Invisible Hand in Economics?, Investopedia, 30.08.2022 (https://www.investopedia.com/terms/i/invisiblehand.asp).

[108] Steve Rolles, GOVERNMENT SELLING STIMULANTS? YES - AND HERE'S WHY, Transform Drug Policy Foundation, 28.10.2020 (https://transformdrugs.org/blog/government-selling-stimulants-yes-and-heres-why).

[109] Editorial: Billboards advertising pot broke Prop. 64's promise. Don't go back on the pledge to protect teens, The Los Angeles Times, 02.01.2022 (https://www.latimes.com/opinion/story/2022-01-02/editorial-billboards-advertising-pot-broke-prop-64s-promise-dont-go-back-on-the-pledge-to-protect-teens).

[110] Single customer view, Wikipedia, 01.10.2022 (https://en.wikipedia.org/wiki/Single_customer_view).

[111] Vitality Plus, John Hancock, 01.10.2022 (https://www.johnhancock.com/life-insurance/vitality.html).

[112] Alcohol-Medication Interactions: Potentially Dangerous Mixes, National Institue on Alcohol Abuse and Alcoholism, 01.10.2022 (https://www.niaaa.nih.gov/health-professionals-communities/core-resource-on-alcohol/alcohol-medication-interactions-potentially-dangerous-mixes).

[113] Jennifer Kim & Kelsey Combs & Jonathan Downs & Frank Tillman, Medication Adherence: The Elephant in the Room, US Pharmacist,

19.01.2018 (https://www.uspharmacist.com/article/medication-adherence-the-elephant-in-the-room).

[114] Jason Rose, Medication Adherence Is Not a Zero-Sum Game, American Journal of Managed Care, 05.04.2022 (https://www.ajmc.com/view/contributor-medication-adherence-is-not-a-zero-sum-game).

[115] Watanabe JH, McInnis T, Hirsch JD. Cost of Prescription Drug-Related Morbidity and Mortality. , Ann Pharmacother, September 2018 (https://pubmed.ncbi.nlm.nih.gov/29577766/).

[116] Prescription Drug Monitoring Programs (PDMPs), Centers for Disease Control and Prevention, 01.10.2022 (https://www.cdc.gov/drugoverdose/pdmp/index.html).

[117] Nneka Chile, Nigerian startups help fight scourge of fake medicines, Reuters, 13.12.2022 (https://www.reuters.com/business/healthcare-pharmaceuticals/nigerian-startups-help-fight-scourge-fake-medicines-2022-01-13/).

[118] Ian Sample, Fake drugs kill more than 250,000 children a year, doctors warn, The Guardian, 11.03.2019 (https://www.theguardian.com/science/2019/mar/11/fake-drugs-kill-more-than-250000-children-a-year-doctors-warn).

[119] Press Release: Up to EUR 4 billion worth of counterfeit pharmaceuticals traded worldwide, European Union Intellectual Property Office (EUIPO), 23.03.2020 (https://euipo.europa.eu/tunnel-web/secure/webdav/guest/document_library/observatory/documents/reports/Trade_in_Counterfeit_Pharmaceutical_Products/Trade_in_Counterfeit_Pharmaceutical_Products_pr_en.pdf).

[120] Tesco Clubcard, Tesco, 01.10.2022 (https://secure.tesco.com/clubcard/about/).

[121] Nectar collection partners, Nectar, 01.10.2022 (https://www.nectar.com/collect).

[122] Home page, FlyBuys, 01.10.2022 (https://www.flybuys.com.au/).

[123] Open-source software development, Wikipedia, 01.10.2022 (https://en.wikipedia.org/wiki/Open-source_software_development).

[124] Home page, Linux, 01.10.2022 (https://www.linux.org/).

[125] Tobacco statistics commentary July 2022, GOV.UK, 31.08.2022

(https://www.gov.uk/government/statistics/tobacco-bulletin/
tobacco-statistics-commentary-april-2022).

[126] Bhutan forbids all tobacco sales, BBC, 17.12.2004 (http://
news.bbc.co.uk/1/hi/world/south_asia/4012639.stm).

[127] Crime groups using illicit tobacco to finance drug trade and
terrorism as cigarette prices soar, says Australian Criminal
Intelligence Commission, ABC News Australia, 18.06.2022 (https://
www.abc.net.au/news/2022-06-18/organised-crime-turning-to-
illicit-tobacco-trade-cigarette-price/101158958).

[128] Services home page, NHS, 01.10.2022 (https://www.nhs.uk/nhs-
services/).

[129] About us, Department of Health & Social Care, 01.10.2022
(https://www.gov.uk/government/organisations/department-of-
health-and-social-care/about).

[130] Understanding the health and care information we collect, NHS,
01.10.2022 (https://digital.nhs.uk/about-nhs-digital/our-work/
keeping-patient-data-safe/how-we-look-after-your-health-and-
care-information/understanding-the-health-and-care-information-
we-collect).

[131] NHS App, NHS, 01.10.2022 (https://digital.nhs.uk/services/nhs-
app).

[132] Nicotine vaping in England: 2022 evidence update summary,
Office for Health Improvement and Disparities, 29.09.2022 (https://
www.gov.uk/government/publications/nicotine-vaping-in-
england-2022-evidence-update/nicotine-vaping-in-england-2022-
evidence-update-summary#chapter-4-vaping-among-adults).

[133] Juul: US bans all products from leading vaping company, BBC,
23.06.2022 (https://www.bbc.co.uk/news/business-61914166).

[134] Selling Tobacco, Association of Convenience Stores, 03.10.2022
(https://www.acs.org.uk/sites/default/files/
acs_selling_tobacco_advice_guide_aw5_18.08.22_aw_lo_res_web.p
df).

[135] Nicotine vaping in England: 2022 evidence update summary,
Office for Health Improvement and Disparities, 29.09.2022 (https://
www.gov.uk/government/publications/nicotine-vaping-in-
england-2022-evidence-update/nicotine-vaping-in-england-2022-
evidence-update-summary#chapter-4-vaping-among-adults).

[136] Astonishing drinking sessions and epic hangovers in the world's

booziest nation, The Daily Telegraph, 28.01.2020 (https://www.telegraph.co.uk/travel/destinations/europe/russia/articles/russians-drink-so-much-alcohol/).

[137] In binge-tolerant Japan, alcoholism not seen as disease, Reuters, 16.11.2009 (https://www.reuters.com/article/us-japan-alcohol/in-binge-tolerant-japan-alcoholism-not-seen-as-disease-idUSTRE5AF0OO20091116).

[138] UNDERSTANDING ALCOHOL LAWS IN KUWAIT: A GUIDE FOR FOREIGNERS, Kuwait Visa, 03.10.2022 (https://kuwaitvisa.com/alcohol-laws-in-kuwait/).

[139] Systembolaget explained, Om Systembolaget, 03.10.2022 (https://www.omsystembolaget.se/english/systembolaget-explained/).

[140] Gray D, Cartwright K, Stearne A, Saggers S, Wilkes E, Wilson M (2018) Review of the harmful use of alcohol among Aboriginal and Torres Strait Islander people. , Australian Indigenous HealthBulletin, 2018 (https://aodknowledgecentre.ecu.edu.au/healthinfonet/getContent.php?linkid=590984).

[141] NT government passes liquor laws to replace Commonwealth Intervention-era alcohol bans in remote communities, ABC News Australia, 18.05.2022 (https://www.abc.net.au/news/2022-05-18/nt-remote-intervention-alcohol-laws-passed-territory-parliament/101077440).

[142] Inside the multi-million chang'aa underworld of Murang'a, The Daily Nation, 27.05.2021 (https://nation.africa/kenya/news/inside-the-multi-million-chang-aa-underworld-of-murang-a-3415052).

[143] Illegal alcohol kills 38 in India after 10 more die in hospital, ABC News Australia, 27.07.2022 (https://www.abc.net.au/news/2022-07-27/illegal-alcohol-kills-38-in-india-after-10-more-die-in-hospital/101275114?utm_campaign=abc_news_web&utm_content=link&utm_medium=content_shared&utm_source=abc_news_web).

[144] Canada becomes second country to legalise Cannabis, The Guardian, 17.10.2018 (https://www.theguardian.com/world/2018/oct/17/cannabis-becomes-legal-in-canada-marijuana).

[145] Philip Olterman, Germany's move to legalise cannabis expected to create 'domino effect', The Guardian, 01.07.2022 (https://www.theguardian.com/world/2022/jul/01/germanys-move-to-

legalise-cannabis-expected-to-create-domino-effect).

[146] Statement by the International Narcotics Control Board on the entry into force of Bill C-45 legalising cannabis for non-medical purposes in Canada, International Narcotics Control Board, 17.10.2018 (https://www.incb.org/incb/en/news/press-releases/2018/statement-by-the-international-narcotics-control-board-on-the-entry-into-force-of-bill-c-45-legalising-cannabis-for-non-medical-purposes-in-canada.html).

[147] Colombia, largest cocaine supplier to U.S., considers decriminalizing, The Washington Post, 20.08.2022 (https://www.washingtonpost.com/world/2022/08/20/colombia-cocaine-decriminalize-petro/).

[148] Martin Jelsma, German cannabis regulation on thin ice, The Transnational Intstitute (TNI), 28.10.2022 (https://www.tni.org/en/article/german-cannabis-regulation-on-thin-ice)

[149] UK crackdown on CBD upends rapidly growing market, Financial Times, 23.04.2022 (https://www.ft.com/content/e4e9d7f5-09d5-429a-bdd1-8d1a35ba6cf9).

[150] Rachel Roubein, Biden's directive on marijuana faces a Catch-22, The Washington Post, 10.10.2022 (https://www.washingtonpost.com/politics/2022/10/10/biden-directive-marijuana-faces-catch-22/)

[151] Jazz agrees $7.2bn deal for British cannabis pioneer GW Pharmaceuticals, Financial Times, 03.02.2021 (https://www.ft.com/content/87e56362-09af-44e3-b2ff-7a7c51f29374).

[152] Harry Sumnall, Medical cannabis and the challenge for regulation of medicines, The Conversation, 06.06.2018 (https://theconversation.com/amp/medical-cannabis-and-the-challenge-for-regulation-of-medicines-97771).

[153] Is marijuana safe and effective as medicine?, National Institute on Drug Abuse, July 2020 (https://nida.nih.gov/publications/research-reports/marijuana/marijuana-safe-effective-medicine).

[154] Eric Pedersen, Medical marijuana cards often sought by existing heavy users, Journal of Studies on Alcohol and Drugs, 04.12.2019 (https://www.sciencedaily.com/releases/2019/12/191204100529.htm).

[155] State and Local Backgrounders: Cannabis Taxes, Urban Institute, 03.10.2022 (https://www.urban.org/policy-centers/cross-center-

initiatives/state-and-local-finance-initiative/state-and-local-backgrounders/marijuana-taxes).

[156] Leighton Woodhouse, How Weed Became the New OxyContin, Tablet Magazine, 31.08.2022 (https://www.tabletmag.com/sections/news/articles/how-weed-became-new-oxycontin-marijuana-psychosis-addiction).

[157] Cannabis and international travel, Government of Canada, 03.10.2022 (https://travel.gc.ca/travelling/cannabis-and-international-travel).

[158] Madelein Kearns, Heavy use of cannabis can lead to psychosis, explain husband-and-wife psychiatrists, National Review, 17.02.2022 (https://www.nationalreview.com/magazine/2022/03/07/reefer-madness/).

[159] Dan Zak, 'Nothing ever ends': Sorting through Rumsfeld's knowns and unknowns, The Washington Post, 01.07.2021 (https://www.washingtonpost.com/lifestyle/style/rumsfeld-dead-words-known-unknowns/2021/07/01/831175c2-d9df-11eb-bb9e-70fda8c37057_story.html).

[160] Clare Wilson, Legalised cannabis in Canada and US hasn't killed illegal market, New Scientist, 24.05.2022 (https://www.newscientist.com/article/2321524-legalised-cannabis-in-canada-and-us-hasnt-killed-illegal-market/).

[161] Sarah Grochowski, Vancouver Sun, 11.02.2022, (https://vancouversun.com/news/local-news/safe-supply)

[162] Daniel Boffey, The Guardian, 18.08.2022, (https://www.theguardian.com/world/2022/aug/18/high-street-dutch-ecstasy-shop-shows-possible-way-for-drug-reform-xtc)

[163] Home page, Qatar Distribution Centre, 03.10.2022 (https://www.qdc.com.qa/).

[164] Rory Jones, Alcohol-Free Saudi Arabia Plans Champagne and Wine Bars at Neom, Wall Street Journal, 22.09.2022 (https://www.wsj.com/articles/alcohol-free-saudi-arabia-plans-champagne-and-wine-bars-at-neom-11663421529).

[165] Toine Pieters, Java Coca and the Dutch Narcotics Industry: An Almost Forgotten 20th C. History of Drugs Story, Points, 10.12.2012 (https://pointshistory.com/2012/12/10/java-coca-and-the-dutch-narcotics-industry-an-almost-forgotten-20th-c-history-of-drugs-story/).

[166] Cannabis (Marihuana) and Expungement Under New York State Law, NYCourts.gov, 03.10.2022 (https://www.nycourts.gov/courthelp/criminal/marihuanaExpunge.shtml).
[167] Lauren Carroll, How the war on drugs affected incarceration rates, The Poynter Institute, 10.07.2016 (https://www.politifact.com/factchecks/2016/jul/10/cory-booker/how-war-drugs-affected-incarceration-rates/).

Acknowledgements

For the last decade or so, lurking on Twitter and following links down proverbial rabbit holes has kept me up to date in drug-related content and general business matters, plus reading the odd book and many periodicals. I apologize profusely for not participating in the Twitter discussion – I hope to start.

A short list of influential and interesting people I have being following or reading the words of are, in alphabetical order by surname: Tom Angell, Azeem Azhar, Alex Berenson, Dame Carol Black, Dr Julian Buchanan, Mattha Busby, Professor Jonathan Caulkins, John Collins, Andrew Cunningham, Max Daly, Jared Dillian, Vanda Felbab-Brown, Dr Henry Fisher, Ann Fordham, Andrew Gallimore, Professor Scott Galloway, Tren Griffin, Kathy Gyngell, Ian Hamilton, Johann Hari, Dr Carl Hart, Peter Hitchens, Professor Keith Humphreys, Jay Jackson, Martin Jelsma, Beau Kilmer, Professor Mark Kleiman, Katya Kowalski, Danny Kushlick, Michelle Lhooq, Tom Lloyd, German Lopez, Alastair Moore, Steve Moore, Ethan Nadelmann, Dr Russell Newcombe, Paul North, Eileen Ormsby, Bryce Pardo, Michael Pollan, Mike Power, Daniel Pryor, Sam Quinones, J S Rafaeli, Jason Reed, Professor Peter Reuter, Steve Rolles, Kevin Sabet, Tony Saggers, Professor Toby Seddon, Michael Shellenberger, Christopher Snowdon, Professor Alex Stevens, Professor Harry Sumnall, Maia Szalavitz, Sanho Tree, Niko Vorobyov, Tom Wainwright, Fred Wilson, and Neil Woods.

You have all been sources of wisdom. Sincere apologies if I have forgotten or overlooked others.

My professional colleagues in technology, marketing and analytics from over the years have helped grow my underlying knowledge regarding what can be done with customer databases and automation, and how commercial organizations can overcome seemingly intractable difficulties if sufficiently motivated.

In the writing of this book, several people have had great patience with me and given their time whilst I have been formulating ideas and trying to turn them into coherent copy. I am very grateful to Murray Barnett, Denis Frize, Vic Kara and Clare MacKenzie for all of their help.

Finally, many thanks to Dan Smith for his superb editing services, helpfully correcting my mangled syntax and grammar.

Printed in Great Britain
by Amazon

12583973R00061